SELECTED
POEMS

1954–1992

This new edition of George Mackay Brown's *Selected Poems* includes more poems than any previous selection. It contains, in addition to poems from his first seven collections and the delightful *Ballad of John Barleycorn*, the texts of three sequences of poems, *Tryst on Egilsay*, *Foresterhill* and *Brodgar Poems*, each of which has so far only been published as a private press book. This work, together with the author's most recent collections, *The Wreck of the Archangel* (1989) and *Following a Lark* (1996), includes all the poems, from more than forty years' work, that he chose to keep in print.

George Mackay Brown was born in Stromness, in Orkney, in 1921 and always lived there. He wrote many plays, poems and stories (*Winter Tales* was published in 1995). In 1988 he was awarded the James Tait Black Memorial Prize for *The Golden Bird*. In 1994 his novel, *Beside the Ocean of Time*, was shortlisted for the Booker Prize and judged Saltire Scottish Book of the Year. He died in April 1996.

D0061935

GEORGE MACKAY BROWN

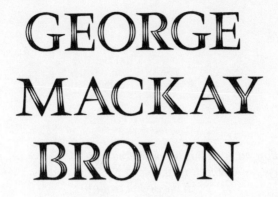

SELECTED POEMS

1954–1992

JOHN MURRAY
Albemarle Street, London

The illustration on the title page depicts the Maeshowe Dragon, a figure carved in Orkney's most famous Neolithic tomb by a Viking early in the twelfth century.

© George Mackay Brown 1954, 1959, 1965, 1971, 1976, 1983, 1988, 1989, 1990, 1991, 1992

First published in 1991
by John Murray (Publishers) Ltd
50 Albemarle Street, London W1X 4BD

New enlarged edition in paperback 1996

British Library Cataloguing in Publication Data
Mackay Brown, George
Selected poems 1954–1992.
I. Title
821

ISBN 0-7195-5624-4

Photoset by Rowland Phototypesetting Ltd
Bury St Edmunds, Suffolk
Printed and bound in Great Britain by
The University Press, Cambridge

To
David Dixon

Contents

Introduction

All the poems in this collection were written in the Orkney islands, off northern Scotland.

More poetry has come out of Orkney than perhaps from any community of comparative size in the world.

The minglings of sea and earth – creel and plough – fish and cornstalk – shore people and shepherds – are the warp and weft that go to make the very stuff of poetry: 'the embroidered cloths' that Yeats wrote about.

More than in cities, the stars in their courses rule our comings and goings. The moon gathers the shoals, the sun sets the well-crusted bread on the tables.

Behind those perennial actions is a rich history, going far back beyond the medieval sagas of Norse Orcadians to the imaginative hewers of stone, the builders of Skarabrae, Brodgar, Maeshowe.

It may be, an Orkney foot was among the first to step ashore on Vinland a thousand years ago.

To the five poems of 'Stations of the Cross' from *Winterfold* have been added for this collection 'A Joyful Mystery' from *Voyages* and 'The House' from *The Wreck of the Archangel* (1989). No other poems from the latter collection feature here because it is still in print.

The book ends with three sequences of poems, each of which I have introduced to the reader. They were all originally published as books: *Tryst on Egilsay* by the Celtic Cross Press, Lastingham, Yorkshire; *Foresterhill* by Babel, Schondorf am Ammersee, Germany; and *Brodgar Poems* by the Perpetua Press, Oxford.

George Mackay Brown
February 1996
Stromness, Orkney

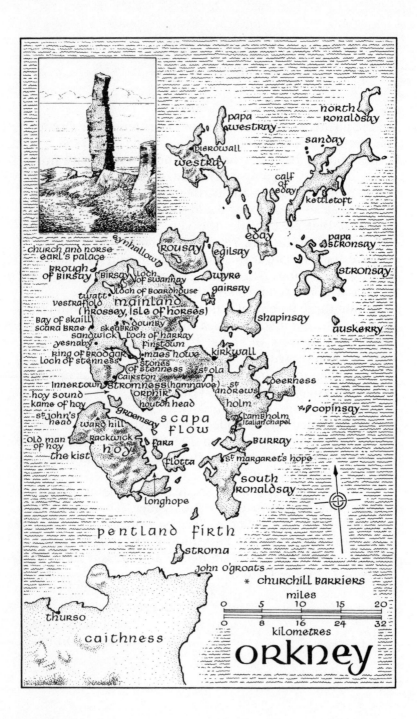

north
ronaldsay

papa
westray

sanday

pierowall

westray

calf
of
eday

kettletoft

church and norse
earl's palace

eynhallow

rousay

egilsay

papa
stronsay

eday

stronsay

brough
of birsay

birsay

loch
of swannay

wyre

gairsay

loch of boardhouse

twatt

vestrafiold

mainland
(hrossey, isle of horses)

shapinsay

auskerry

bay of skaill

skeabrae

dounby

scara brae

sandwick

loch of harray

finstown

yesnaby

ring of brodgar

maes howe

kirkwall

loch of stenness

stones
of stenness

st ola

cairston

innertown

stromness (hamnavoe)

st
andrews

deerness

hoy sound

orphir

copinsay

kame of hoy

houton head

holm

st john's
head

ward hill

graemsay

scapa
flow

lamb holm
italian chapel

old man
of hoy

rackwick

fara

burray

the kist

hoy

flotta

st margaret's hope

longhope

south
ronaldsay

pentland firth

stroma

john o'groats

* churchill barriers

thurso

miles

0	5	10	15	20
0	8	16	24	32

kilometres

caithness

orkney

SELECTED
POEMS

1954–1992

The Storm

What blinding storm there was! How it
Flashed with a leap and lance of nails,
    Lurching, O suddenly
    Over the lambing hills,

Hounding me there! With sobbing lungs
I reeled past kirk and alehouse
    And the thousand candles
    Of gorse round my mother's yard,

And down the sand shot out our skiff
Into the long green jaws, while deep
    In summer's sultry throat
    Dry thunder stammered.

Swiftly the sail drew me over
The snarling Sound, scudding before
    The heraldic clouds now
    Rampant all around.

The sea – organ and harps – wailed miserere;
Swung me in fluent valleys, poised
    On icy yielding peaks
    Hissing spume, until

Rousay before me, the stout mast
Snapped, billowing down helpless sail.
    What evil joy the storm
    Seized us! plunged and spun!

And flung us, skiff and man (wave-crossed, God-lost)
On a rasp of rock! . . . The shore breakers,
    Stained chancel lights,
    Cluster of mellow bells,

Crossed hands, scent of holy water . . .
The storm danced over all that night,
    Loud with demons, but I
    Safe in Brother Colm's cell.

Next morning in tranced sunshine
The corn lay squashed on every hill;
    Tang and tern were strewn
    Among highest pastures.

I tell you this, my son: after
That Godsent storm, I find peace here
    These many years with
    The Gray Monks of Eynhallow.

The Exile

So, blinded with Love
He tried to blunder
Out of that field
Of floods and thunder.

The frontiers were closed.
At every gate
The sworded pitiless
Angels wait.

There's no retreat.
The path mounts higher
And every summit
Fringed with fire.

The night is blind,
Dark winds, dark rains:
But now his blood
Pours through his veins,

His hammer heart
Thuds in his breast
'What Love devises,
That is best',

And he would not turn,
Though the further side
Dowered his days
With fame and pride.

What though his feet
Are hurt and bare?
Love walks with him
In the menacing air.

The frontiers sealed;
His foot on the stone;
And low in the East
The gash of dawn.

Song: Further than Hoy

Further than Hoy
the mermaids whisper
through ivory shells
a-babble with vowels

Further than history
the legends thicken
the buried broken
vases and columns

Further than fame
are fleas and visions,
the hermit's cave
under the mountain

Further than song
the hushed awakening
of country children
the harp unstroked

Further than death
your feet will come
to the forest, black forest
where Love walks, alone.

The Old Women

Go sad or sweet or riotous with beer
Past the old women gossiping by the hour,
They'll fix on you from every close and pier
An acid look to make your veins run sour.

'No help,' they say, 'his grandfather that's dead
Was troubled with the same dry-throated curse,
And many a night he made the ditch his bed.
This blood comes welling from the same cracked source.'

On every kind of merriment they frown.
But I have known a gray-eyed sober boy
Sail to the lobsters in a storm, and drown.
Over his body dripping on the stones
Those same old hags would weave into their moans
An undersong of terrible holy joy.

The Death of Peter Esson
Tailor, Town Librarian, Free Kirk Elder

Peter at some immortal cloth, it seemed,
Fashioned and stitched, for so long had he sat
Heraldic on his bench. We never dreamed
It was his shroud that he was busy at.

Well Peter knew, his thousand books would pass
Gray into dust, that still a tinker's tale
As hard as granite and as sweet as grass,
Told over reeking pipes, outlasts them all.

The Free Kirk cleaves gray houses – Peter's ark
Freighted for heaven, galeblown with psalm and prayer.
The predestined needle quivered on the mark.
The wheel spun true. The seventieth rock was near.

Peter, I mourned. Early on Monday last
There came a wave and stood above your mast.

Hamnavoe

My father passed with his penny letters
Through closes opening and shutting like legends
    When barbarous with gulls
    Hamnavoe's morning broke

On the salt and tar steps. Herring boats,
Puffing red sails, the tillers
    Of cold horizons, leaned
    Down the gull-gaunt tide

And threw dark nets on sudden silver harvests.
A cart-horse at the sweet fountain
    Dredged water, and touched
    Fire from steel-kissed cobbles.

Hard on noon four bearded merchants
Past the pipe-spitting pier-head strolled,
    Rosy with greed, chanting
    Their slow grave jargon.

A tinker keened like a tartan gull
At cuithe-hung doors. The brass
    Tongue of the bellman fore-tolled
    'Coon concert!' . . . 'Cargo of English coal!'. . .

In the Arctic Whaler three blue elbows fell,
Regular as waves, from beards spumy with porter,
    Till the amber day ebbed out
    To its black dregs.

The boats drove furrows homeward, like ploughmen
In blizzards of gulls. Gaelic fisher girls
    Flashed knife and dirge
    Over drifts of herring,

And boys with penny wands lured gleams
From the tangled veins of the flood. Houses went blind
    Up one steep close, for a
    Grief by the shrouded nets.

The kirk, in a gale of psalms, went heaving through
A tumult of roofs, freighted for heaven. Ploughboy
    And milklass tarried under
    The buttered bannock of the moon.

He quenched his lantern, leaving the last door.
Because of his gay poverty that kept
    My seapink innocence
    From the worm and black wind;

And because, under equality's sun,
All things wear now to a common soiling,
    In the fire of images
    Gladly I put my hand
    To save that day for him.

The Lodging

The stones of the desert town
Flush; and, a star-filled wave,
Night steeples down.

From a pub door here and there
A random ribald song
Leaks on the air.

The Roman in a strange land
Broods, wearily leaning
His lance in the sand.

The innkeeper over the fire
Counting his haul, hears not
The cry from the byre;

But rummaging in the till
Grumbles at the drunken shepherds
Dancing on the hill;

And wonders, pale and grudging,
If the strange pair below
Will pay their lodging.

Elegy

The Magnustide long swords of rain
  Quicken the dust. The ploughman turns
    Furrow by holy furrow
      The liturgy of April.
  What rock of sorrow
Checks the seed's throb and flow
Now the lark's skein is thrown
    About the burning sacrificial hill?

Cold exiles from that ravished tree
  (Fables and animals guard it now)
    Whose reconciling leaves
      Fold stone, cornstalk and lark,
    Our first blood grieves
That never again her lips
Flowering with song we'll see,
    Who, winged and bright, speeds down into the
                                              dark.

Now let those risers from the dead,
  Cornstalks, golden conspirators,
    Cry on the careless wind
      Ripeness and resurrection;
    How the calm wound
Of the girl entering earth's side
Gives back immortal bread
    For this year's dust and rain that shall be man.

Chapel between Cornfield and Shore, Stromness

Above the ebb, that gray uprooted wall
Was arch and chancel, choir and sanctuary,
A solid round of stone and ritual.
Knox brought all down in his wild hogmanay.

The wave turns round. New ceremonies will thrust
From the thrawn acre where those good stones bleed
Like corn compelling sun and rain and dust
After the crucifixion of the seed.

Restore to that maimed rockpool, when the flood
Sounds all her lucent strings, its ocean dance;
And let the bronze bell nod and cry above
Ploughshare and creel; and sieged with hungry sins
A fisher priest offer our spindrift bread
For the hooked hands and harrowed heart of Love.

Daffodils

Heads skewered with grief
Three Marys at the cross
(Christ was wire and wax
festooned on a dead tree)

Guardians of the rock,
their emerald tapers touch
the pale wick of the sun
and perish before the rose
bleeds on the solstice stone
and the cornstalk unloads
peace from hills of thorn

Spindrifting blossoms
from the gray comber of March
thundering on the world,
splash our rooms coldly with
first grace of light, until
the corn-tides throb, and fields
drown in honey and fleeces

Shawled in radiance
tissue of sun and snow
three bowl-bound daffodils
in the Euclidean season
when darkness equals light
and the world's circle shudders

13

down to one bleeding point
Mary Mary and Mary
triangle of grief.

Shipwreck

Paul grounded at Braga, a gull on his shoulder.
The milkmaids wrung him dry.
He lay that night at the fire of Lifia
And then moved inland
And keeps pigs on a black hill.
  Jan put a cut of tobacco in his teeth
When the *Maggi* struck.
They found him at the end of the kirk
Near dawn, out of the gale,
Squirting poison among the tombstones.
  For Gregory was much grief in the crofts.
The sea did not offer him with green hands
To the seven dark shawls.
His bones fouled no net or slipway.
With small diagonals crabs covered him.
  Two storms and a dove later
A man with a limpet pail
Turned a gold swathe among seaweed.
That was the hair
Of Robin, weaver of nets, in a warp of ebb.
  Peero said when the first lump of salt
Fell through wrenched timbers,
'Now it seems I can never
Hang a brass chain at my belly
Or sit in the council
Or go among doors with the holy cards'. . .
The gray lumps fell and fell and stopped his mouth.

Peter was three years getting home from the wreck.
He found his feet at Houton.
The ale-house there kept him a week.
He stayed at Gair for harvest,
Drowned and drunk again with broken corn,
Then shipped at Hamnavoe
For the blue fish, the whales, the Davis Straits
And casks of hellfire Arctic rum.
He stood dry in his door at last.
Merrag wore a black shawl.
He read his own tombstone that evening.
 For Donald the way was not long.
His father had a dozen horse at Skaill
But Donald loved the dark net.
Indeed for Donald the day and the way were not long.
Old men had said,
'Such skill at Greek and physics and poetry
Will bring this Donald fame at last.'
But for him the day was not long.
His day was this long –
Sixteen years, four months, and two days.

Culloden: The Last Battle

The black cloud crumbled.
  My plaid that Morag wove
In Drumnakeil, three months before the eagle
Fell in the west, curled like the gray sea hag
Around my blood.
  We crouched on the long moor
And broke our last round bannock.
  Fergus Mor
Was praying to every crossed and beaded saint
That swung Iona, like the keel of Scotland,
Into the wrecking European wave.
Gow shook his flask. Alastair sang out
They would be drunker yet on German blood
Before the hawk was up. For 'Look', cried he,
'At all the hogsheads waiting to be tapped
Among the rocks'. . .
  Old iron-mouth spilled his brimstone,
Nodded and roared. Then all were at their thunders,
And Fergus fell, and Donald gave a cry
Like a wounded stag, and raised his steel and ran
Into the pack.
  But we were hunters too,
All smoking tongues. I picked my chosen quarry
Between the squares. Morag at her wheel
Turning the fog of wool to a thin swift line
Of August light, drew me to love no surer
Than that red man to war. And his cold stance

Seemed to expect my coming. We had hastened
Faithful as brothers from the sixth cry of God
To play this game of ghost on the long moor.
His eyes were hard as dice, his cheek was cropped
For the far tryst, his Saxon bayonet
Bright as a wolf's tooth. Our wild paths raced together,
Locked in the heather, faltered by the white stone,
Then mine went on alone.
        'Come back, come back',
Alastair cried.
        I turned.
        Three piercing shapes
Drifted about me in the drifting smoke.
We crossed like dreams.
        This was the last battle.
We had not turned before.
        The eagle was up
And away to the Isles.
        That night we lay
Far in the west. Alastair died in the straw.
We travelled homeward, on the old lost roads,
Twilight by twilight, clachan by weeping sheepfold.

My three wounds were heavy and round as medals
Till Morag broke them with her long fingers.

Weaving, she sings of the beauty of defeat.

Horseman and Seals, Birsay

On the green holm they built their church.
There were three arches.
They walked to the village across the ebb.
From this house they got milk.
A farmer cut and carted their peats.
Against their rock
Fishermen left a basket of mouthing silver.
They brought the gifts of heaven
To the new children and the suffering shapes.
They returned to the island
And mixed their bell with the seven sounds of the sea.
Eight times a day
They murmured their psalms in that steep pasture.

A horseman stood at the shore, his feet in seaweed.
He could not cross over.
The sea lay round the isle, a bright girdle.
His voice scattered in the vastness
Though from shore to shore pierced cries of gull and
                                                petrel.
What did the horseman want?
Perhaps an old man in the parish was sick,
Or he wanted a blessing on his ship,
Or he wished to argue a point in theology.
From shore to shore they blessed him.
They trooped under the arch for nones.

After the psalms the horseman was still there,
Patient in the seaweed.
The sea shone higher round the skerry.
And the abbot said, 'Cormac, you are the carpenter,
A blessed occupation.
And tomorrow you will beg some boards and nails
And you will build a little boat,
So that we do not need to keep horsemen waiting on the
                                                    other shore
Who are in need of God'. . .

And while the boat was building under the crag
Paul gathered whelks.
From the cold triangular pools he gathered handfuls
And put them in his basket.
He sang *Dominus Pascit Me*, gathering whelks in the ebb.
Twenty seals lay on the skerry.
They turned their faces towards the psalm.
The brother sang for them also,
For the seals with their beautiful gentle old men's faces.
Then the ebb subtracted one sound
From the seven-fold harmony of ocean.
The tide lay slack, between ebb and flowing, a slipped
                                                    girdle.
Paul gathered whelks and sang
Till the flood set in from the west, with a sound like harps,
And one by one the seals entered the new water.

The Abbot

Here at Innertun we have seven brothers.
Havard was a shepherd
In Hoy, that huddle of blue shoulders.
In the tavern there
He broke the back of a loud fisherman.
He has given his fifty sheep to the widow,
To the three orphans his green hill.
At Innertun now, he weaves our coats.

At Rinansay, Einar was a butterfly
Over a tangled harp.
The girls miss him in that low island.
Now when candles are lit
For matins, in the warp of winter,
He drifts, our gray moth
Among the woven monotonies of God.

Sigurd sailed to Iceland, a boy,
And lost an arm there.
He was with Leif on the Greenland voyage.
He bought a Galway horse, sire of thirty
And sailed home from Norway
With tusks of walrus, proper embellishment
For hilt and helmet and ale-cup.
'Too old now', said Sigurd
'For any port but the blue of heaven,
I teach the brothers shipwit'.

We have a field at Innertun
That was full of stones last April.
Plenty of lobsters, goat milk
At our fasting tables.
Then Erling rode from Birsay, love-torn.
He laid a plough on our acre.
He gives us bannocks and new ale.

You would not wish to have seen
The *Gothenberg* at the crag
Like a hare in the cold jaw of a wolf.
You would not wish to have seen
Gulls over blind shapes on the sand.
From the timbers we made a new door
And the Swedish boy
Has Latin enough to answer the priest now.

Rolf whistled down the wild hawk.
He brought twelve rampant foals
From the hill Greenay,
Gale shapes, to the horse fair at Hamnavoe.
He put a ring in the bull's nose,
And said in a circle of drunk whalers
'There is a time to finish with beasts
And to strive with angels'.
His knee was at our line of knees next morning.

This day is a day of sheaves at Innertun
And five crisp circles.
A yellow wind walks on the hill.
The small boats in the Sound
Pluck this brightness and that from the nets.
Our cow watched a black field in March,
And deepening greens, all summer.
Today she cries over a sudden radiance,
The clean death of corn.
Christ, crofter, lay kindly on this white beard
Thy sickle, flail, millstone, fires. . .
They shout across the broken gold.
The boy has found a lark's nest in the oats.

The Poet

Therefore he no more troubled the pool of silence.
But put on mask and cloak,
Strung a guitar
And moved among the folk.
Dancing they cried,
'Ah, how our sober islands
Are gay again, since this blind lyrical tramp
Invaded the Fair!'

Under the last dead lamp
When all the dancers and masks had gone inside
His cold stare
Returned to its true task, interrogation of silence.

Farm Labourer

'God, am I not dead yet?' said Ward, his ear
  Meeting another dawn.
    A blackbird, lost in leaves, began to throb
And on the pier
    The gulls stretched barbarous throats
    Over the creels, the haddock lines, the boats.
  His mortal pain
    All day hung tangled in that lyrical web.
'Seventy years I've had of this', said Ward,
  'Going in winter dark
    To feed the horse, a lantern in my fist,
Snow in my beard,
    Then thresh in the long barn
    Bread and ale out of the skinflint corn,
  And such-like work!'
    And a lark flashed its needle down the west.

Old Fisherman with Guitar

A formal exercise for withered fingers.
   The head is bent,
      The eyes half closed, the tune
Lingers
      And beats, a gentle wing the west had thrown
      Against his breakwater wall with salt savage lament.

So fierce and sweet the song on the plucked string,
   Know now for truth
      Those hands have cut from the net
The strong
      Crab-eaten corpse of Jock washed from a boat
     One old winter, and gathered the mouth of Thora to his
                                      mouth.

The Year of the Whale

The old go, one by one, like guttered flames.
   This past ewe-shiver
      Tammag the bee-man has taken his blank mask
      To the honeycomb under the hill;
         Corston who ploughed out the moor
      Unyoked and gone; and I ask
   Is Heddle lame, that famous dancer wherever
      Bow to strings was laid?
The kirkyard is full of their names
      Chiselled in stone. Only myself and Yule
         In the ale-house now, speak of the great whale
                                             year.

This one and that provoked the bull-belling waves
   With a careless pass,
      Or probing deep through the snow-burdened hill
      Resurrected a flock.
         Or passed from fiddles to ditch
      By way of the quart and the gill,
All night lay tranced with corn, but stirred to face
      The brutal stations of bread;
While those who tended their lives
      Like sacred lamps, chary of oil and wick,
         Died in the fury of one careless match.

Off Scabra Head the lookout sighted a school
   At the first light.
      A meagre year it was, limpets and crows
      And brief mottled grain.
         Everything that could float
         Circled the school. Ploughs
      Wounded those wallowing lumps of thunder and
                                                night.
         The women crouched and prayed.
Then whale by whale by whale
      Blundering on the rock with its red stain
      Crammed our winter cupboards with oil
                                    and meat.

Trout Fisher

Semphill, his hat stuck full of hooks
   Sits drinking ale
      Among the English fishing visitors,
   Probes in detail
         Their faults in casting, reeling, selection of flies.
'Never', he urges, 'do what it says in the books'.
      Then they, obscurely wise,
        Abandon by the loch their dripping oars
And hang their throttled tarnish on the scale.

'Forgive me, every speckled trout',
   Says Semphill then,
      'And every swan and eider on these waters.
   Certain strange men
         Taking advantage of my poverty
Have wheedled all my subtle loch-craft out
      So that their butchery
        Seem fine technique in the ear of wives and
                                  daughters.
   And I betray the loch for a white coin'.

Hamnavoe Market

They drove to the Market with ringing pockets.

Folster found a girl
Who put lipstick wounds on his face and throat,
Small and diagonal, like red doves.

Johnston stood beside the barrel.
All day he stood there.
He woke in a ditch, his mouth full of ashes.

Grieve bought a balloon and a goldfish.
He swung through the air.
He fired shotguns, rolled pennies, ate sweet fog from a
stick.

Heddle was at the Market also.
I know nothing of his activities.
He is and always was a quiet man.

Garson went three rounds with a negro boxer,
And received thirty shillings,
Much applause, and an eye loaded with thunder.

Where did they find Flett?
They found him in a brazen circle,
All flame and blood, a new Salvationist.

A gypsy saw in the hand of Halcro
Great strolling herds, harvests, a proud woman.
He wintered in the poorhouse.

They drove home from the Market under the stars
Except for Johnston
Who lay in a ditch, his mouth full of dying fires.

The Hawk

On Sunday the hawk fell on Bigging
    And a chicken screamed
    Lost in its own little snowstorm.
And on Monday he fell on the moor
    And the Field Club
    Raised a hundred silent prisms.
And on Tuesday he fell on the hill
    And the happy lamb
    Never knew why the loud collie straddled him.
And on Wednesday he fell on a bush
    And the blackbird
    Laid by his little flute for the last time.
And on Thursday he fell on Cleat
    And peerie Tom's rabbit
    Swung in a single arc from shore to hill.
And on Friday he fell on a ditch
    But the questing cat,
    That rival, rampant, fluttered his flame.
And on Saturday he fell on Bigging
    And Jock lowered his gun
    And nailed a small wing over the corn.

The Ballad of John Barleycorn,
The Ploughman, and the Furrow

As I was ploughing in my field
The hungriest furrow ever torn
Followed my plough and she did cry
'Have you seen my mate John Barleycorn?'

Says I, 'Has he got a yellow beard?
Is he always whispering night and morn?
Does he up and dance when the wind is high?'
Says she, *'That's my John Barleycorn.*

One day they took a cruel knife
(O, I am weary and forlorn!)
They struck him at his golden prayer.
They killed my priest, John Barleycorn.

They laid him on a wooden cart,
Of all his summer glory shorn,
And threshers broke with stick and stave
The shining bones of Barleycorn.

The miller's stone went round and round,
They rolled him underneath with scorn,
The miller filled a hundred sacks
With the crushed pride of Barleycorn.

A baker came by and bought his dust.
That was a madman, I'll be sworn.
He burned my hero in a rage
Of twisting flames, John Barleycorn.

A brewer came by and stole his heart.
Alas, that ever I was born!
He thrust it in a brimming vat
And drowned my dear John Barleycorn.

And now I travel narrow roads,
My hungry feet are dark and worn,
But no one in this winter world
Has seen my dancer Barleycorn.'

I took a bannock from my bag.
Lord, how her empty mouth did yawn!
Says I, 'Your starving days are done,
For here's your lost John Barleycorn.'

I took a bottle from my pouch,
I poured out whisky in a horn.
Says I, 'Put by your grief, for here
Is the merry blood of Barleycorn.'

She ate, she drank, she laughed, she danced.
And home with me she did return.
By candle-light in my ingle-nook
She wept no more for Barleycorn.

The Five Voyages of Arnor

1   THE FIVE VOYAGES OF ARNOR

I, Arnor the red poet, made
Four voyages out of Orkney.

The first was to Ireland.
That was a viking cruise.
Thorleif came home with one leg.
We left Guthorm in Ulster,
His blood growing cold by the saint's well.
Rounding Cape Wrath, I made my first poem.

Norway hung fogs about me.
I won the girl Ragnhild
From Paul her brother, after
I beat him at draughts, three games to two.
Out of Bergen, the waves made her sick.
She was uglier than I expected, still
I made five poems about her
That men sing round the benches at Yule.
She filled my quiet house with words.

'The cousin Sweyn is howe-laid in Iceland
After his man-slaying'. . .
They put an axe in my hand, the edge turned north.
Women in black stood all about me.
We sailed no further than Unst in Shetland.
We bade there a month.

We drank the ale and discussed new metres.
For the women, I reddened the axe at a whale wound.

I went the blue road to Jerusalem
With fifteen ships in a brawling company
Of poets, warriors, and holy men.
A hundred swords were broken that voyage.
Prayer on a hundred white wings
Rose every morning. The Mediterranean
Was richer by a hundred love songs.
We saw the hills where God walked
And the last hill where his feet were broken.
At Rome, the earl left us. His hooves beat north.

Three Fridays sick of the black cough
Tomorrow I make my last voyage.
I should have endured this thing,
A bright sword in the storm of swords,
At Dublin, Micklegarth, Narbonne.
But here, at Hamnavoe, a pillow is under my head.
May all things be done in order.
The priest has given me oil and bread, a sweet cargo.
Ragnhild my daughter will cross my hands.
The boy Ljot must ring the bell.
I have said to Erling Saltfingers, *Drop my harp*
Through a green wave, off Yesnaby,
Next time you row to the lobsters.

The twenty brothers of Eynhallow
Have made a figure of Our Lady.
From red stone they carved her
And set her on a headland.
There spindrift salts her feet.
At dawn the brothers sang this
    Blessed Lady, since midnight
    We have done three things.
    We have bent hooks.
    We have patched a sail.
    We have sharpened knives.
    Yet the little silver brothers are afraid.
    Bid them come to our net.
    Show them our fire, our fine round plates.
    Per Christum Dominum nostrum
    Look mildly on our hungers.

The codling hang in a row by the wall.
At noon the brothers sang this
    Holy Mother, Una the cow
    Gives thin blue milk.
    Where is the golden thread of butter?
    The stone in the middle of the glebe
    Has deep black roots.
    We have broken three ploughs on it.
    Per Christum Dominum nostrum
    Save Una from the axe,
    Our dappled cow with large eyes.

The girls go by with pails to the byre.
At sunset the brothers sang this
      Sweet Virgin, the women of Garth
      Bring endless gifts to Brother Paul.
      They put an egg in his palm,
      They lay peats in his cowl.
      One neck is long as spilling milk.
      Brother Paul is a good lad.
      Well he brings wine and word to the priest.
      At midnight he sits by a white candle.

Paul has gnarled knees at the stone.
At midnight the brothers sang this
      Queen of Heaven, this good day
      There is a new cradle at Quoys.
      It rocks on the blue floor.
      And there is a new coffin at Hamnavoe.
      Arnor the poet lies there,
      Tired of words and wounds.
      In between, what is man?
      A head bent over fish and bread and ale.
      Outside, the long furrow.
      Through a door, a board with a shape on it.

Guard the ploughs and the nets.

Star of the Sea, shine for us.

Ox

To Thorstein the Ox, I give and bequeath these furrows,
The hawk above, the seal below,
The worn runes over the lintel
> *Ingibiorg tallest of women*
> *carried wine to the traveller*
Let the fire watch from the hill, Thorstein.
Scour the axe at the grindstone.
Beat the plough into edges.
I expect Bui from Ireland
Now that his cheek has the bronze curl.
His father opened the quarry.
His father took the hawk on his wrist.
His father sang to the curious seals.
His father had fair dust to carry under the lintel
Ingibiorg, tallest of women.
His father rode down to the ships.
Then one morning
His father lay crooked in seaweed,
A cold man among red swathings.
> Hoof and scarecrow are Thorstein's,
Scythe, flail, quernstone, forge.
So dowered, the ox in the furrows
May quench those Irish axes.
To Helga his wife, ale-kirn and griddle.

Dove

To the Eynhallow kirk, my fishing-boat *Skua*,
The sail and the oar also.
Erling, our holy prodigal, is there,
Gaunt with heavenly bread.
His net is a bunch of various holes,
A thing of laughter to fish.
Lost in prayer, the hands of the brothers
Are clumsy with ploughshares.
Rooted in praise, their tongues
Compel corn and oil
From the seven ox-dragged seasons.
Their queen is a stone woman,
Their lord a scarecrow with five red tatters.
Mild as a tree of doves,
Bui's wrath is no more to them
Than a painted hawk on a sail.
My net on those long robes
Who call the codling 'little silver brothers'
Even as they suck the bones clean
All the brightening days of Lent.

Rose

I do not forget thee, my Sigrid.
He carried thee off to Barra
(Thee and thy thirteen Aprils)
Einar thy man. Too soon
That prow unlocked the horizon.
 Thy father is quiet now
Who once bore fire to the castles,
And as for thy brothers, one
Has a skull square as an ox,
And Erling glides in a trance
Through bell and psalm and secret,
A cold mouth in the godstreams.
 What can I leave thee? Thou hast
Horizons of whale and mermaid
Far in the west, a hall,
Three ships in Cornwall and Ulster, trading,
A young son with black curls
And five horses in the meadow.
Arnor has sailed to the quarries in Eday
With chisel and harp.
That stone is red as fire, roses, blood.
I pay well for my verses.
'Cut a deep rune for Sigrid, Arnor'.
Irishmen will read it perhaps
Over a fated lintel,
One fragrant stone among blackened stones.

Carol

In the first darkness, a star bled.

The war of cloud and summit, other wounds.
Hills cupped their hands
And the rain shone over knuckles of rock and dropped to
                                                    the sources.
Precious that well-hoard.
The priests gathered in secret jars
Lustrations for the passionate and the dead.

You were blessed, young tree
With one apple.
Far on you must bear the five godwounds, prefigured and
                                                                red.

The deer runs on, runs on, swiftly runs on
Before bird and arrow,
Then bends, obedient to the arrow, its branching head.

A hunter's hand has broken the wild grape
To stain and seed.
And the hunter's hill opened with a green sound,
A stalk of corn,
And the blacksmith took from his forge a powerful blade.

Now this, a cry in our atom-and-planet night –
A child wailing,
A child's cry at the door of the House-of-Bread.

Kirkyard

A silent conquering army,
The island dead,
Column on column, each with a stone banner
Raised over his head.

A green wave full of fish
Drifted far
In wavering westering ebb-drawn shoals beyond
Sinker or star.

A labyrinth of celled
And waxen pain.
Yet I come to the honeycomb often, to sip the finished
Fragrance of men.

Runes from a Holy Island

Press-Gang
A man-of-war enchanted
Three boys away.
Pinleg, Windbag, Lord Rum returned.

Hierarchy
A claret laird,
Seven fishermen with ploughs,
Women, beasts, corn, fish, stones.

Harpoonist
He once riveted boat to whale.
Frail-fingered now
He weaves crab prisons.

Books
No more ballads in Eynhallow.
The schoolmaster
Opens a box of grammars.

Skerries
A fanged treeless island.
On shipwrecked wood
Men die, feast, cry sunwards.

The Chapel of The Visitation
> Before the unuttered Christ stone
> A new arch,
> Two bending women, a stone kiss.

Ruined Chapel
> Among scattered Christ stones
> Devoutly leave
> Torn nets, toothache, winter wombs.

Saint
> A starved island, Cormack
> With crossed hands,
> Stones become haddock and loaf.

Easter
> Friday, dayspring, a pealing cockerel.
> Haul west, fishermen,
> With flushed violent mouths.

Lost
> An island without roads.
> Ikey the tinker
> Stood throat-deep in the bog.

Dove and Crow
> A preacher broke our dove-stone.
> Sermons, crowflocks,
> Blackened furrow and shore.

Whale
> Whale, give needles and oil.
> Winter hands
> Must sew shrouds by lamplight.

Fish and Corn
> Our isle is oyster-gray,
> That patched coat
> Is the Island of Horses.

Runes from the Island of Horses

Winter
> Three winter brightnesses –
> Bridesheet, boy in snow,
> Kirkyard spade.

Barn Dance
> Fiddler to farm-girls, a reel,
> A rose,
> A tumult of opening circles.

Farm Girl
> Spinster, elder, moth
> Quiz till dawn
> The lamp in Merran's window.

Kirkyard
> Pennies for eyes, we seek
> Unbearable treasure
> Through a wilderness of skulls.

Mirror
> Ikey unpacked a flat stone.
> It brimmed
> With clouds, buttercups, false smiles.

Witch

Three horsemen rode between the hills
And they dismounted at Greenhill.
Tall they stooped in at the door.
No long time then
Till Wilma came out among them, laughing.
The fishless fishermen watched from the shore.
She sat behind the second dark rider.
They left the valley at noon.
And Wilma did not come back that day
Nor the next day
Nor any day at all that week.
And the dog barked lonely at Greenhill
And the girls took turns at milking her cow.
(One took the froth from her vat.)
The laird sent word
At the end of winter, to James of Reumin
That on Candlemas Friday
He should sail his dinghy to Kirkwall.
He sailed the *Lupin* to the red church.
And there at a steep place, Gallowsha,
Among tilted bottles, fists, faces
– A cold drunken wheel –
James saw the hangman put the red shirt on Wilma.

He sailed back smouldering
From the fire, the rum, the reproaches.
The dog of Greenhill
Barked in the throat of the valley.
And next morning
They launched their boat at the dawn with a wild shout,
The three unlucky fishermen.

A Reel of Seven Fishermen
(Bride, Mother, Fisherman)

Her hands put flame among the peats.
The old one took three fish from the smoke.
Cod off The Kist, drifting, an undersea song.

She sank buckets in the cold burn.
The old one broke a bannock in three.
A withershin step. A cry! A steeple of wings.

She turned quernstones, circle on circle.
The Book lay open, two white halves.
Twelve arms sought the cold dancer.

She squeezed oil in the black lamps.
The old one spread the kirkyard shirt.
Twelve feet beat on the hill, a dance.

Her hands brought fish and ale to the table.
The old one soughed, a winter thorn.
Twelve feet stood in the door, a dance.

Sea streamed like blood on the floor.
They shrieked, gull mouths.
Then bride and mother bowed to the black music.

Taxman

Seven scythes leaned at the wall.
Beard upon golden beard
The last barley load
Swayed through the yard.
The girls uncorked the ale.
Fiddle and feet moved together.
Then between stubble and heather
A horseman rode.

Buonaparte, the Laird, and the Volunteers

I, Harry Cruickshank, laird in Hoy
Being by your lordships bidden
To supply from my lands in Rackwick, Hoy,
For His Majesty's ships-of-war
Seven hale hearty willing seamen
Upon payment of the agreed bounty, two guineas,
Did thereupon name
> John Stewart at Greenhill, fisherman,
> James Stewart at Greenhill, crofter,
> William Mowat at Bunertoon, fisherman,
> Andrew Sinclair at Mucklehouse, fisherman,
> Thomas Thomson at Crowsnest, fisherman,
> James Robb at Scar, fisherman,
> James Leask at Reumin, crofter and fisherman
All unmarried, save for Wᵐ Mowat,
Who got wife and cow from Graemsay at the fall of the
> year
And James Robb, a widower –
The rest all young men in their strength.
I duly rode with officers to the valley
To give notice of impressment to the said men
But found them removed
And the old people dumb and cold as stones.
One said, they were gone fishing, very far out –
Faroe, Rockall, Sulisker.
Another, to the horse-market in Caithness.
Another, 'the trows were taen them aneath the hill'. . .

Upon the Sabbath following
I came to the kirk of Hoy secretly with four officers
Between the sermon and the last psalm.
We took John and James Stewart in the kirk door.
They were quiet enough after the minister spoke with
                                                   them
(By this, they will be in Portsmouth.)
It is certain, my lords,
Robb and Thomson are in the caves.
Andrew Sinclair, fisherman, Mucklehouse
Listed in Hamnavoe for the Davis Straits
On the whaler *Tavistock*
(We found his mark and name in the agent's book).
And Mowat ferried himself to Graemsay
With wife and cow
And there hacked three fingers from his right hand
And stifled the ruin with tar.
As for Leask, he is broken with troll-music.
He lies day-long in the back of the bed,
Dark hollows about his skull.
The old woman says, 'in a decline, consumption.'
She stitches away at a shroud.
But like enough, the guns being silent
And Buonaparte down,
He will make his customary furrows along the hill.
A dozen old men are left in the valley.
Last week, your lordships,
I observed two women rowing to the lobsters.
Ploughmen next April will have shrill voices.

The Laird

Once it was spring with me
     Stone shield and sundial
Lily and lamb in the Lenten grass;
The ribs of crag and tree
        Resurrecting with birds;
In the mouths of passing crofter and fisher lass
Shy folded words.

Then one tall summer came
     Stone shield and sundial
The year of gun and rod and hawk;
The hills all purple flame;
        The burn supple with trout;
Candle-light, claret, kisses, witty talk,
Crinoline, flute.

Autumn, all russet, fell
     Stone shield and sundial
I wore the golden harvest beard.
I folded my people well
        In shield and fable.
Elders and councillors hung upon my word
At the long table.

Now winter shrinks the heart
     Stone shield and sundial
I'd quit this withered heraldry

To drive with Jock in his cart
    To the hill for peat,
Or seed a field, or from clutches of sea
Take a torn net.

Crofter's Death

They will leave the quiet valley,
The daylight come.
Skulls, bones have been dug
From a loaded tomb.
Seventy years burdened and sunbound, they
                    might see in the kirkyard
Their honeycomb.
They will carve a name, some years
On withered stone.
The hill road will drag them back
To hunger again.
In the valley are creels for baiting,
A field to be sown.

Peat Cutting

And we left our beds in the dark
And we drove a cart to the hill
And we buried the jar of ale in the bog
And our small blades glittered in the dayspring
And we tore dark squares, thick pages
From the Book of Fire
And we spread them wet on the heather
And horseflies, poisonous hooks,
Stuck in our arms
And we laid off our coats
And our blades sank deep into water
And the lord of the bog, the kestrel
Paced round the sun
And at noon we leaned on our tuskars
– The cold unburied jar
Touched, like a girl, a circle of burning mouths
And the boy found a wild bees' comb
And his mouth was a sudden brightness
And the kestrel fell
And a lark flashed a needle across the west
And we spread a thousand peats
Between one summer star
And the black chaos of fire at the earth's centre.

Ikey Crosses the Ward Hill to the Spanish Wreck

Because of the Spanish wreck I tackled the hill.
I heard of the apples,
Winekegs, mermaids, green silk bale upon bale.

My belly hollowed with hunger on the hill.
From Black Meg's rig
I borrowed a chicken and a curl or two of kale.

We both wore patches, me and that harvest hill.
Past kirk and croft,
Past school and smithy I went, past manse and mill.

On the black height of the hill
I lay like a god.
Far below the crofters came and went, and suffered,
                                    and did my will.

I wrung a rabbit and fire from the flank of the hill.
In slow dark circles
Another robber of barrows slouched, the kestrel.

Corn and nets on the downslope of the hill.
The girl at Reumin
Called off her dog, poured me a bowl of ale.

I found no silk or brandy. A bit of a sail
Covered a shape at the rock.
Round it the women set up their soundless wail.

Ploughman and Whales

The ox went forward, a black block, eyes bulging,
The mouth a furnace.
Tammag went forward, cursing.
The plough wavered between them.
And the gulls plagued Tammag, a whirl of savage snow
On the field of the sun.
Twice the plough struck stone,
A clang like a bell
Between the burning hills and the cold sea.
Tammag clawed his shoulder. He cursed.
And the ox belched lessening flame.
Six furrows now and a bit . . .
Suddenly Tammag heard it, low thunder
Far in the firth,
And saw blue surging hills, the whales
On trek from ocean to ocean.
They plunged, they dipped, they wallowed,
They sieved a million small fish through their teeth.
The sun stood at the hill, a black circle.
The shore erupted with men and boats,
A skirl of women,
Loud dogs, seaward asylums of gulls.
The ox stood in the seventh furrow
In a dream of grass and water.
'Tammag!' the boatmen cried. 'Tammag!'
Tammag wiped his silver face on his sleeve,

He yelled at the ox. The plough wavered. They
                                                stumbled on.
They tore from the black sun
Loaf, honey-comb, fleece, ale-jar, fiddle.

Love Letter

To Mistress Madeline Richan, widow
At Quoy, parish of Voes, in the time of hay:
    The old woman sat in her chair, mouth agape
    At the end of April.
    There were buttercups in a jar in the window.

    The floor is not a blue mirror now
    And the table has flies and bits of crust on it.

    Also the lamp is broken.

    I have the shop at the end of the house
    With sugar, tea, tobacco, paraffin
    And, for whisperers, a cup of whisky.

    There is a cow, a lady of butter, in the long silk grass
    And seven sheep on Moorfea.

    The croft girls are too young.
    Nothing but giggles, lipstick and gramophone records.

    Walk over the hill Friday evening.
    Enter without knocking
    If you see one red rose in the window.

Haddock Fishermen

Midnight. The wind yawing nor-east.
A low blunt moon.
Unquiet beside quiet wives we rest.

A spit of rain and a gull
In the open door.
The lit fire. A quick mouthful of ale.

We push the *Merle* at a sea of cold flame.
The oars drip honey.
Hook by hook uncoils under The Kame.

Our line breaks the trek of sudden thousands.
Twelve nobbled jaws,
Gray cowls, gape in our hands,

Twelve cold mouths scream without sound.
The sea is empty again.
Like tinkers the bright ones endlessly shift their ground.

We probe emptiness all the afternoon;
Unyoke; and taste
The true earth-food, beef and barley scone.

Sunset drives a butcher blade
In the day's throat.
We turn through an ebb salt and sticky as blood.

More stars than fish. Women, cats, a gull
Mewl at the rock.
The valley divides the meagre miracle.

The Laird's Falcon

The falcon on the weathered shield
　　Broke from his heraldic hover
　　To drift like a still question over
The fecund quarterings of the field.

Doves in that dappled countryside,
　　Monotones of round gray notes,
　　Took his bone circle in their throats,
Shed a mild silence, bled, and died.

All autumn, powered with vagrant blood
　　(But shackled to a silken call)
　　He paced above the purple hill,
His small black shadow tranced the wood.

Steadfast himself, a lord of space,
　　He saw the red hulk of the sun
　　Strand in the west, and white stars run
Their ordered cold chaotic race;

Till from lucidities of ice
　　He settled on a storied fist,
　　A stone enchantment, and was lost
In a dark hood and a sweet voice.

Sea Runes

Five Crags
    The five black angels of Hoy
    That fishermen avoid –
    The Sneuk, The Too, The Kame, Rora, The Berry.

Elder
    Charlag who has read the prophets
    A score of times
    Has thumbed the salt book also, wave after wave.

Crofter-Fisherman
    Sea-plough, fish-plough, provider
    Make orderly furrows.
    The herring will jostle like August corn.

Shopkeeper
    Twine, sea stockings, still to pay
    And Howie trading
    Cod for rum in the ale-house.

New Boat
    We call this boat *Pigeon*.
    Go gentle, dove
    Among skuas, easterlies, reefs, whalebacks.

Fishmonger
    The fishmonger stood at the rock
    With bits of dull silver
    To trade for torrents of uncaught silver.

The Scarecrow in the Schoolmaster's Oats

Hail, Mister Snowman. Farewell,
Gray consumptive.

Rain. A sleeve dripping.
Broken mirrors all about me.

A thrush laid eggs in my pocket.
My April coat was one long rapture.

I push back green spume, yellow breakers,
King Canute.

One morning I handled infinite gold,
King Midas.

I do not trust Ikey the tinker.
He has a worse coat.

A Hogmanay sun the colour of whisky
Seeps through my rags.
I am – what you guess – King Barleycorn.

A Child's Calendar

No visitors in January.
A snowman smokes a cold pipe in the yard.

They stand about like ancient women,
The February hills.
They have seen many a coming and going, the hills.

In March, Moorfea is littered
With knock-kneed lambs.

Daffodils at the door in April,
Three shawled Marys.
A lark splurges in galilees of sky.

And in May
Peatmen strike the bog with spades,
Summoning black fire.

The June bee
Bumps in the pane with a heavy bag of plunder.

Strangers swarm in July
With cameras, binoculars, bird books.

He thumped the crag in August,
A blind blue whale.

September crofts get wrecked in blond surges.
They struggle, the harvesters,
They drag loaf and ale-kirn into winter.

In October the fishmonger
Argues, pleads, threatens at the shore.

Nothing in November
But tinkers at the door, keening, with cans.

Some December midnight
Christ, lord, lie warm in our byre.
Here are stars, an ox, poverty enough.

Beachcomber

Monday I found a boot –
Rust and salt leather.
I gave it back to the sea, to dance in.

Tuesday a spar of timber worth thirty bob.
Next winter
It will be a chair, a coffin, a bed.

Wednesday a half can of Swedish spirits.
I tilted my head.
The shore was cold with mermaids and angels.

Thursday I got nothing, seaweed,
A whale bone,
Wet feet and a bad cough.

Friday I held a seaman's skull,
Sand spilling from it
The way time is told on kirkyard stones.

Saturday a barrel of sodden oranges.
A Spanish ship
Was wrecked last month at The Kame.

Sunday, for fear of the elders,
I smoke on the stone.
What's heaven? A sea chest with a thousand gold coins.

Old Man

'Before the cuckoo puts his two notes over the burn –
The wings crowd south
Flight by fall
The birds return

'What with rheumatics, asthma, and whisky the price it is –
The sap sinks
Shower by spring
The waters rise

'Peedie* Tam will have my plough, and my fiddle, and
oars.'
Come, dancer, go
Step by circle
The reel endures.

* *peedie – small*

70

Roads

The road to the burn
Is pails, gossip, gray linen.

The road to the shore
Is salt and tar.

We call the track to the peats
The kestrel road.

The road to the kirk
Is a road of silences.

Ploughmen's feet
Have beaten a road to the lamp and barrel.

And the road from the shop
Is loaves, sugar, paraffin, newspapers, gossip.

Tinkers and shepherds
Have the whole round hill for a road.

Butter

What's come of my churning? The van-man, he took
seven pounds, and a basket of warm eggs, for jam,
sugar, tea, paraffin. I gave the tinkers a lump,
to keep the black word from our byre. I put some
on the damp peats, to coax a flame. I swear the
cat has a yellow tongue. There was only a scrape
for the fisherman's bannock, like a bit of sun on
a dull day. The old cow is giving me a mad look.

72

The Coward

All Monday he sat by the fire, Stoney the fisherman
Loud with a hoast,*
Till Jean bought a guaranteed nostrum from the van.
In terror at the black stuff in the bottle,
When Jean was out, luring eggs from the hen,
He coughed his way to the noust†
And launched the *Belle* with a lurch and a rattle
Into a sea
Shaken with spasms as loud and green as he.
He came back late
With a score of lobsters, sillocks like stars, a skate
As wide and bright as the moon
And devil the hoast.
He felt as rich as the laird as he landed his creels.
But there, a patient Penelope on the coast,
Stood Jean with a spoon
And the phial that, warts to consumption, cured all ills.

* *hoast – cough*
† *noust – boat shelter*

73

Hill Runes

Thirst
    Horse at trough, thrush in quernstone,
    The five ploughmen
    Much taken up with pewter.

Elder
    Andrew who has read the gospel
    Two or three times
    Has quizzed the clay book also, furrow by furrow.

Smithy
    The forge flames, the hammerings, glowings,
    End one way –
    A cold nail on an anvil.

Kirkyard
    Between stone poem and skull
    April
    Touches rat, spade, daffodil.

Tractor
    The horsemen are red in the stable
    With whisky and wrath.
    The petrol-drinker is in the hills.

The Big Wind

The big wind trundled our pail, a clanging bell
Through the four crofts,
Broke the clean circles of wave and gull,
Laid the high hay in drifts,
Beat down the stones of the dead,
Drove the *Beagle* aground,
Whirled rose-petals, spindrift, round Merran's head,
And set three hen-houses (cockerels raging aloft)
                              on the crested Sound.
The kestrel stood unmoving over the hill.

Dead Fires

At Burnmouth the door hangs from a broken hinge
And the fire is out.

The windows of Shore empty sockets
And the hearth coldness.

At Bunertoon the small drains are choked.
Thrushes sing in the chimney.

Stars shine through the roofbeams of Scar.
No flame is needed
To warm ghost and nettle and rat.

Greenhill is sunk in a new bog.
No bending woman
Blows russet wind through squares of ancient turf.

The Moss is a tumble of stones.
That one black stone
Is the stone where the hearth fire was rooted.

In Crawnest the sunken hearth
Lit many a story-tranced mouth,
Old seamen from the clippers with silken beards.

The three-toed pot at the wall of Park
Is lost to woman's cunning.
A slow fire of rust eats the cold iron.

The sheep drift through Reumin all winter.
Sheep and snow
Blanch fleetingly the black stone.

From that good stone the children of the valley
Drifted lovewards
And out of labour to the lettered kirkyard stone.

The fire beat like a heart in each house
From the first cornerstone
Till they led through a sagged lintel the last old one.

The poor and the good fires are all quenched.
Now, cold angel, keep the valley
From the bedlam and cinders of A Black Pentecost.

The Golden Door: Three Kings

1

I unlatched the jade door.
Worms were breeding silk,
A girl fingered a loom.
I entered the golden door
(There my throne stood, withering).
I passed through rooms
Of flowers, flagons, chessboards
And a room with a fountain.
At the top of the black spiral
A wise one said, 'Majesty,
Three nights now we have seen this planet.
The time is come
For exile, the tent in the desert.'

2

What wandered about the star streets
Last night, late?
It knocked for shelter at doors of gold, like a lost boy.
My heart was bruised with the image.
I am waiting now at sunset, again, with my charts.
I had perhaps drunk too much midnight wine.

3

When the lawmen have gone
Before the girl enters
With water and a lamp
I sit at the window.
The stars come, each after other.
'I am the bringer of Dew.'
'I am the Dove.'
'I am the Swarm of Bees.'
'I am the Grain of Dust from the Floor of Heaven.'
'I am the Emerald.'
'I am the Temple Lamp.'
I greet those faithful
Who troop to my dark window.
What should I say
To this one, intruder and stranger?
He has stood there two nights
And is silent still.
I imagine a title,
'Keeper of the Door of Corn.'
And a word, 'Come.'

Yule

Castle to forest, more wind, and the roads drifted.
We followed the map as best we could.
We came at noon to the marked tree,
A gray gnarled column.
The sergeant shouted. Our axes flashed. They bit.
We struck out pieces of bark and bole.
We laboured like men in a siege, among whirls of snow,
But root was one with leaf-node still
In the first red seepings of sunset.
      In the village windows, that twilight,
Tinsel stars glittered.
There were chains of coloured tissue and paper lanterns.
Under the street lamp, a chasteness of carolling mouths.
Then the village slept, unblessed by the winter tree.
The sky was a hushed river of light.
Flagons gleamed in firelight at the inn.
Three strangers came, burdened. They were shown rooms.
'No word of this at the castle,' said Blok at midnight.
'Some childishness, star and snowman and crib,
Crippled our arms today.
In March we'll be back. The peasants will have their tree.'

A *Poem for* Shelter

Who was so rich
He owned diamonds and snowflakes and fire,
The leaf and the forest,
Herring and whale and horizon –
Who had the key to the chamber beyond the stars
And the key of the grave –
Who was sower and seed and bread
Came on a black night
To a poor hovel with a star peeking through rafters
And slept among beasts
And put a sweet cold look on kings and shepherds.

But the children of time, their rooftrees should be strong.

Tea Poems

1 *CHINAMAN*

Water, first creature of the gods.
It dances in many masks.
    For a young child, milk.
    For the peasant, honey and mud.
    For lovers and poets, wine.
    For the man on his way to the block, many well-
                              directed spits.
    For an enemy, mixings of blood.
    For the Dragon-god, ichor.
    For a dead friend, a measure of eye-salt.

A courteous man is entertaining strangers
Among his goldfish and willows.
The musician sits in the pavilion door
(His flute is swathed in silk.)
An urn is brought to the table by girls.
This is the water of offered friendship.
Notice the agreeable angle of pouring,
The pure ascending columns of vapour,
The precise arrangement of finger and bowl and lip.
Birds make all about those sippers and smilers ceremonies
                          of very sweet sound.

Midnight. Measured musical cold sea circles.

The yawl struck suddenly!

Oars wrapped the boat in a tangled web.

The boy cried out – Smith gagged him with tarry fingers.

It was no rock, not the fearful face of Hoy.

The boat spun back from pliant timbers.

A maze of voices above us then.

Our skipper growled, 'Where's your light?'

(A lantern was to hang in the cross-trees

For half-an-hour after midnight.

In the Arctic Whaler, that had been harped on well.)

'You comm too litt,' a Dutchman said,

The words like a fankle of rusted wire.

'A sticky ebb,' said Smith

'And it's only twenty-past-twelve. Lower down

Twelve kegs rum, tobacco as much as you've got,

A horn of snuff for the laird. Have you rolls of silk?'

He drew out silver, rang it in his fist like a bell.

Now we could see green-black curves of hull,

Cropped heads hung over the side,

Even the mouth that was torturing the language.

'Fif box tea, bess China.'

With fearful patience our skipper told on his fingers

The smuggler's litany:

Silk, rum, tobacco. The florins chimed in his fist.

'Rum. Tobacco. Silk. That was the understanding.'

Smith swore to God not he nor any Orkneyman

Would risk rope or irons for women's swill.

He pleaded. He praised. He threatened.

Again the stony voice from the star-web above. 'Tea.

Noding but China tea. For silver. Fif box.'

Drank Mrs Leask, sticking out her pinkie.
Drank Mrs Spence, having poured in a tinkle-tinkle of
                                    whisky (*I've such a bad cold!*)
Drank Mrs Halcrow, kissing her cup like a lover.
Drank Mrs Traill, and her Pekinese filthied the floor
                        with bits of biscuit and chocolate.
Drank Mrs Clouston, through rocky jaws.
Drank Mrs Heddle, her mouth dodging a sliver of
                                                lemon.
Drank Bella the tea wife, who then read
   engagements, letters, trips and love in every
                            circling clay hollow.

April the Sixteenth

What did they bring to the saint?
The shepherds a fleece.
That winter many lambs were born in the snow.

What did the dark ones bring?
To Magnus the tinkers have brought
A new bright can. Their hammers beat all night.

What have they brought to the saint?
A fishless fisherman
Spread his torn net at the wall of the church.

And the farm boys offered
A sweetness, gaiety, chasteness
Of hymning mouths.

The women came to their martyr
With woven things
And salt butter for the poor of the island.

And the poor of the island
Came with their hungers,
Then went hovelwards with crossed hands over the hill.

Twelfth-Century Norse Lyrics of Rognvald Kolson, Earl and Saint

[1]

The Accomplishments of an Earl

Chessboard, tiltyard, trout-stream
Know my sweet passes.
Old writings are no mystery to me
Nor any modern book.
Ski across winterfold flashes.
Deep curves I make with arrow and oar.
I know the twelve notes of a harp.
At the red forge
My clamorous shadow is sometimes rooted.

[2]

Merchant Ship

Five weeks our keel lay choked
In Grimsby mudflats.
Lugworm and silt, a foul grey honey.
Unfurl, white sail
Eastwards, over the loose waves,
A questing skua
To the hard rock of Bergen.

[3]

The Westray Monks

Sixteen walkers about the church,
Heads bare as stone,
Long striders, deep-voiced, rough-handed.
'Brother wind, gentle sister raindrops' –
That's what they call this black whirl of storm.
They haven't a sword between them.
Here they come, in procession,
Demure and harmless as girls.

[4]

A Shipwreck in Shetland

Help and *Arrow*, those slender seekers,
Scatter to a hundred boards.
Women may weep for that
But the poets
Are glad of shipwrecks many a winter night.
The sailors, shamed,
Will ravel their sea-skills with a tougher thread.

I've swallowed mouthfuls of sea.
They gladdened me more
Than the best wine or mead.
The sea sings like a girl over my half-drowned feet.
With shivering mouth
I draw the hammered snake-ring from my finger.
I pledge myself to Our Lady of the Waves.

In a princely coat, stiff with runes and dragons,
I leapt from the wreck.
Cold now, sea-insulted,
I shiver at a Shetland fire.
With tattered sealskin
The women cancel my nakedness.

Einar, laird, though at your board
You give room to no stranger
Unless the chief stranger come, the Earl,
Yet set out horns
And ring your hearth with benches.
Tonight I am riding
To visit your unpopular house.

[5]
Love Songs to the Lady Ermengarde of Narbonne
Your hair, lady
Is long, a bright waterfall.
You move through the warriors
Rich and tall as starlight.
What can I give
For the cup and kisses brought to my mouth?
Nothing.
This red hand, a death-dealer.

The summer mouth of Ermengarde
Commands two things –
A sea of saga-stuff, wreckage, gold,
As far as Jordan,
And later, at leaf-fall,
On patched homing wings
A sun-dark hero.

White as snow
White as silver
The lady,
A beauty all whiteness,
A kindness
Red as wine.
Another redness, fire
About the castle,
A sharp whiteness, swords.

[6]

In praise of Audun, the first warrior to board the African ship
Audun the Red
Was the earliest reaper
In this harvest.
Black sheaves
Fell on the dromond.
Flame-bearded Audun
Was complete gules.
Erling's Audun
Through fire and blood
Bound his red harvest.

[7]
Jerusalem
We stand here, shriven,
A hundred warmen lustred with penance,
In each hand
Assoiled from murders, bordels, thievings now
A leaf of palm.
Footsteps, free and fated, turn
To the fourteen redemptive lingerings
And the hill marked † with this sign.

[8]
A Mass at Sea
We left our shares to rust
On a northern hill,
Exchanged oxen for green and blue tramplers!
Poet, peasant, priest,
One ark of pilgrims
Out of the dragon sea, a seeking
Into the lucencies of Christ.
(Salt furrows we make
Under your headlands, Byzantium.)
Sin darkens the grain-hold.
We have branded their coasts with rage and lust,
The old dragon-breath.
No end of sorrow, soultroth, seeking, still.
Kyrie, Christe, Kyrie eleison
The Golden Harvester
Comes out to grace, with robe and ring, the swineherd.

Vikings: Two Harp-songs

1 BJORN THE SHETLANDER SAILS TO LARGS, 1263

I am a farmer from Yell in Shetland.
Bjorn my mother called me.
I grew among seals and clouds and birds and women.
The men came home in the ships for harvest
With wounds on them and bits of silver.
One year my father did not come home.
The sea has him, off Lindisfarne.
I learned to lift alehorn and hawk that winter.
I can handle horse or boat,
Useful crafts for a man to know,
And am thought to be a good chess-player
And passable on the harp.
Next year, if I live that long
My beard will have a fine golden curl to it.
Perhaps Thora will love me then.
I have never been further south than Whalsay.
Is it true, what the vikings say –
Wine-skins, ivory, black faces south of Spain
And kirks colder than sea-caves?
This is good, to have seen fifteen summers.
Tomorrow with Paul and Sverr my brothers
I sail for Scotland.
A thousand sea-borne swords, a golden mask.

2   THE NEW SKIPPER

Arn, Thorvald, Sven, Paul, Grettir, Harald
The *Sea Wolf* is out of the shed, new tar on her hull.
The rollers are under the keel.
The women have put ale, salt meat, and bread on board.
As soon as the wave runs clean from Birsay
We will leave the Orkneys behind us,
The scarred hills and the creeled sounds,
And tonight we will anchor at the mouth of a Scottish
                                                river.
Our voyage lies east this year.
We have heard of such towns – Aberdeen, Grimsby,
                                                London,
And the merchants who live in tall houses.
The churches have had enough of our swords
And the girls who weave their words into curse or spell.
Our voyage does not lie west this spring
Among holiness and drifts of rain.
There are few chalices left in those islands.
It is time the merchants knew about us.
We will be back in time for the corn harvest.
You women, see that the scythes are sharp and the barns
                                                swept,
And the ale thick with honey.
We are tired of broken coast-lines.
This summer we deal in wool and useful currency.
They are not too beautiful, the girls in the east.

The Escape of the Hart
(an acrostic for S.C.)

Suddenly, on the hill, pursuit and flight!
Taut bows, a hound across the dawn, the stag's
Enormous leap to pacify the arrow.
Love,
Let the white beast move in power this evening across
                         the hunter's hill, breaking through
All tangled desires, dancing wounds, to a secret
                                  water.

Cold it was in the corrie that morning,
A harsh rain. We drew the prince
Round by the eyrie, the thunders of new water.
The Saxons lay in the next glen.
We signed our bread with holy crosses. Then,
Red on the moor, through shrouds and prisms of fog,
                         we saw the hunters
Issue like beads of blood.
God keep our prince, our beautiful stag, from such
                          danger again!
He looked at them with a cold eye.
Then rain let down its silver enchanted walls.

Eynhallow: Crofter and Monastery

I rent and till a patch of dirt
Not much bigger than my coat.
I keep a cow and twelve swine
And some sheep and a boat.
                    Drudgings, stone

The name of my wife is Hild.
Hild has a bitter tongue.
She makes passable butter and ale.
Her mouth brims and brims with bairnsong.
                    Driftings, stone

What's winter? A thousand stars,
Shrinkings of snow, an empty pail.
All summer I go, a drenched ox
Between the plough and the flail.
                    Drudgings, stone

I say a prayer when I remember.
When the bishop comes to bless his flock
I tell my sins and give him a fish.
Once I saw a sealwoman on a rock.
                    Driftings, stone

Twelve bald heads have come to this island.
They divide the day with Terce and Laud.
Herring are 'the little silver brothers'.
Like dust-of-gold they sift each clod.
                    Dancings, stone

Stations of the Cross

1 FROM STONE TO THORN

Condemnation
> The winter jar of honey and grain
> Is a Lenten urn.

Cross
> Lord, it is time. Take our yoke
> And sunwards turn.

First Fall
> To drudge in furrows till you drop
> Is to be born

Mother of God
> Out of the mild mothering hill
> And the chaste burn.

Simon
> God-begun, the barley rack
> By man is borne.

Veronica
> Foldings of women. Your harrow sweat
> Darkens her yarn.

Second Fall
> Sower-and-Seed, one flesh, you fling
> From stone to thorn.

Women of Jerusalem
> You are bound for the Kingdom of Death. The enfolded
> Women mourn.

Third Fall
> Scythes are sharpened to bring you down,
> King Barleycorn.

The Stripping
> Flails creak. Golden coat
> From kernel is torn.

Crucifixion
> The fruitful stones thunder around,
> Quern on quern.

Death
> The last black hunger rages through you
> With hoof and horn.

Pietà
> Mother, fold him from those furrows,
> Your broken bairn.

Sepulchre
> Shepherd, angel, king are kneeling, look,
> In the door of the barn.

2   PILATE

Cool water over my fingers flowing.

The upstart

Had ruined a night and a morning for me.
I thrust that stone face from my door.

I was told later he measured his length
Between the cupid and the rose bush.
The gardener told me that later, laughing.

And that a woman hung upon him like a fountain.

What is it to me, who helps this 'king'
Or strikes him down?
I reduced majesty to a driven shadow.

Another woman stood between him and the sun,
A tree, sifting light and shadow across his face.

Outside the tavern
It was down with him once more, knees and elbows,
Four holes in the dust.

More women then, a gale of them,
His face like a scald
And they moving about him, a tumult of shadows
                                        and breezes.

He clung close to the curve of the world.

The king had gone out in a purple coat.
Now the king
Wore only rags of flesh about the bone.

(I examined cornstalks in the store at Joppa
And discovered a black kernel.

Of the seven vats shipped from Rhodes
Two had leaked in the hold,
One fell from the sling and was broken.)

And tell this Arimathean
He can do what he likes with the less-than-shadow.

No more today. That business is over. Pass the seal.

3 *THE STONE CROSS*

At dawn Havard sighted a hill in Ulster.
'A point to west,' said the helmsman. 'There the hive is.
There the barren kingdom of drones.'

We sailed past cave and cormorant and curragh.
We anchored under a stone cross at noon.

Creatures came down to meet us
With stony heads, voices like insects, raised hands.

They murmured, 'Mother', 'Sancta Maria', 'Our Lady'
But that hostess was not to be seen.

Brother Simon drew me from sea to rock.
He made a cross of gray air between us.

It was a household of men only.
A boy offered to wipe salt from our foreheads.

'Havard, it is time to make a start now.'
Havard flashed his axe in the face of a brother.

Then women began to screech from the crag above,
Gaelic keenings and cursings.

A dozen eunuchs fell beside the porch.
The boy made a dove of his two hands.

We entered a cave of wax and perfumes.
Mund took a silver cup from a niche.

Cold tinklings like nails
Took us to nothing – a crust, a red splash.

Soon that hive was all smoke and stickiness.

We brought a fair cargo down to the *Skua*.
The abbot had called that treasure 'moth-food'.

Sunset. Sharing of spoils. A harp-stroke.
Soon I drifted into the stone of sleep.

4   *SEA VILLAGE: SHETLAND*

There he rides now. Look. The laird.
A brace of grouse to the Manse.
One hand on the rein long and white and scented.

Every boat in the voe his, and the gear.
He fixes the price of the catch.
But a certain fisherman has laid his own keel.

The store? That's his too. After dark
It's a shebeen, with a crock
Of peatsmoke whisky. A man can drink till he falls.

The fisherman's mother bides here, a good woman.
Every tramp, with her, is a prince.
It's her boy, Ollie Manson, that's building the boat.

The whole parish forbidden to help him.
But Simon left his threshing
And brought hammer and rivets down to the rock.

And Vera, when he humped over the tarpot
Came with a jar from the burn.
His face flashed once in the gray water.

A black lamp in a window there. Look.
A good skipper once,
All but ruined with aquavit and rum.

The five widows of the *Hopeful*
In this one threshold,
Rock-gathered, like stormbirds, head into wind.

Socialist books, that was the start of it.
I blame the dominie.
Paine and Blatchford, they'll bring him down.

It'll end with lawmen and prison.
They'll burn the thatch,
The mother will sit under a bare roof-tree.

No need to tell you, with the clang and reek,
Who's shuttered here.
The blacksmith hammering nails for the Hall.

That's it now, on the noust, the *Equality*.
'The yawl is finished!'
The yawl is finished. More than a yawl is finished.

L. Smith, Joiner. Always a coffin on hand.
Never a smile on Lowrie
But when a window goes blind in some croft.

Up there, among the cornfields, the kirk
Cold as a sunk creel.
On a Sabbath, sea voices shake the stone.

5   CARPENTER

'Workman, what will you make on the bench today?'
I was going to hammer a crib for Mary.

I went into a multitude of green shadows, early.
I came to the marked tree at last.

I struck the root with my axe.
It groaned in the dust.

Mary came over the fields to call me to dinner –
One glance among trembling branches.

The woodman dragged it into the village,
A length of gnarls and knots. A bad bargain.

Could it yield, perhaps,
A wheel for spinning of coarse yarn?

(It looked ancient enough, that tree, to have carried the
                                                    seed
Of Adam's Fall.)

I could drag out of the thrawn-ness, I suppose,
A board
Or wash-tub or shelf or churn, for the village women
– Never a crib for Mary's boy.

I let it lie
Among the adzes and squares, in a dazzle of sawdust, all
                                                  morning.

I lopped, later, boughs and branches and bark.

Then a centurion came
And ordered, in the governor's name, a gallows.

I sent him elsewhere.
That's all it's good for, though, a tree of death.

Mary stood in the door, curling cold hands like leaves
Round the fruit of her womb.

'Hurry,' she said. 'Let the saw sing,
Soon it will be time for the cradle to rock my boy.'

He had left the tree, the ass, the apple basket.

We turned our faces back to the town.
One man had seen a boy traded for silver,
Gone on with camels then.

A boy had stood at a stone with bruised knees.

Boy after boy, blithe lissom corn-high faces,
Never the lonely sun-look.

We got to Simon's yard at noon.
He had lingered there.
On had danced, playing shepherds, reeds at his mouth.

At Veronica's he had asked for a basin.
She showed us the towel,
A splotch of happy dust and blood at the centre.

Three beggars sat with locked tongues
In the next village.
A stick wrote in the dust.

Women at a bleach-green stretched long fingers.
An hour since, city-bound
Young hair indeed had streamed past.

We circled, slowly, a foot-print in dew.

A cloud,
Red tatters, the drained heart of the day.

Star scatter (grains of dead salt). I laid
Skull beside breathing skull.

We took our skulls at dawn to the Dove Gate.
The market-place a tumult of ghosts and skulls.

Skulls traded, mimed, looked out of windows, smiled.
Ghosts came and flickered and went.

We drew, hollow-eyed, at noon, to the temple.
Doctors of law read tombstones
Under dew and drift of apple blossom.

7   *THE HOUSE*

In such granite rock
How shall a house be built? Let them see to it.

After the rains, men dug to the hard rock.
The carpenter strove with the roof-tree.

A scaffolding fell.
Three drunk labourers were given their books.

She who was to grace the finished house,
Baker of loaves, keeper of the loom,
She stood in a web of rafters.

The work languished. Another mason was sent for,
A man of solid reputation.

One hot day a girl took a jar of ale to the site.

Thunder in August wrenched an iron lattice,
A sudden brilliance out of the banked gray and purple.

Masons laid a lintel, a cold stone.
Women stood here and there.
They gossiped. They nodded. They said, 'House of sorrow'.

Before harvest labourers climbed down from the eaves.

A diviner went in a slow dance.
Rock was struck to a tumult of bright circles.

Dazzle – first snow – on planed and sanded pine.
At the time of crocuses
Carpenters put the last nail in the staircase.

Painters, tilers, men with snibs and latches –
Ladders and planks and buckets borne away.
The architect's voice from the balcony, 'It is finished'.

The woman came again with daffodils.
She set a jar on the sill.

And still the house echoed like a tomb
Till the village women arrived with gifts.
They stayed to eat the cakes from the new-lit hearth.

Seal Island Anthology, 1875

Market Day
  He came back from the town
  With news
  Of fighting in Russia
  And red things like tatties (apples)
  And sixpenny spectacles –
  His eyes were big as an ox.

Minister
  Polish twelve boots.
  Run
  To the well for water
  To splash faces in:
  Kirstag has seen
  The boat rowing from Rousay,
  A black column in it.

Fishing Boats in Fog
  Rob's boat is in, blinded,
  A thin catch.
  The *Teeack* had nothing. (Mist, sun-pearl.)
  Rob, did you see Tam and Mansie?
  What ghost is this
  Driven by insane pewter swirls?

Widower
   Old Stephen three winters now
   Has spoken to none
   But his cat
   And the spider at the back of his bed
   And himself
   And to a stone in the kirkyard
   With thirteen names
   (The last cut sharp and deep).

Croft Wife
   Make ale. Make
   Butter, cheese, bread (small suns).
   Make
   Every summer the nine-fold rounding
   Moon shape.
   Make fire. Make a star
   In the frozen well.

Dead Faces
   When I saw the first star-coldness
   I was a child.
   I have seen faces the sea has eaten
   And pain-clenched faces
   And faces like flowers, gathered.
   I have seen the face of a dead man
   Who still
   Laughs, bargains, boasts, at the pier.

Rain
    A gray hoof whirled at the sun, splinterings
    Of blue and yellow and orange.
    I felt
    Corn cells, underfoot, gorging.
    A trout
    Flashed from the salt into brief sweetness.

Blacksmith
    As the wild bees
    Forge
    Sweetness under a stone
    As roots in darkness
    Hammer up
    Clusters of the may-flower

    Since the lass of Clett
    Was here
    With her father's plough to patch
    I go with sun pieces
    Between forge and wincing anvil.

Letter
    Dear Parents, at last
        You hear from me.
            The day
    I went to Kirkwall for feeing
        A kind-spoken sailor
    Asked me to broach a bottle in his cabin.
        I woke among wastes of sea.
  I am well. I write this
    At a table of black gold-ringed hands.

Wisdom

    Say, 'I have seen the migrant sail dwindling west.'
    Say, 'Golden hand among fallen stalks.'
    Say, 'We ate seaweed and limpets one spring.'
    Say, 'I have closed ten eyes, or a dozen eyes.'
    Say, 'The laird gets younger and greedier.'
    Say, 'They increase, the things beyond utterance.'
    Then it's time
    To leave dark lamp and folded breath
    And row old into the dayspring.

American

    Sander is home from gold-mines and railroads
    Twanging
    Music from the root of his nose.

Gossip about a Girl

    'She goes like the burdened bee'. . .
    'The slut. The shame'. . .
    'She has the face of a bairn that keeps a bird in the cage
                                of her hands'. . .
    'The moon wheel turns. The ninth round knits with the
            wheel of the sun, as burn is meshed into ocean'. . .
    'She goes, in secret, migrant to cranny'. . .
    'That my hidden silver (it rots) might be hers'. . .

Nocturne
    The candle draught-flung. I hit
    The shadow
    At the pane with my pillow.
    I hit it with nails and feet.
    I hit the stranger
    (That smelt like Willie of Gorse)
    Again and again
    With the rose of my mouth.

Pig Sticker
    The sweet pigling
    Squandered
    His life in shower on shower of roses.

    The bairns
    Put drained faces against the wall.

    He washed, later
    In gray water, the last beast-petal off.

Snow
    The young men went
            Here and there, secret
        At star-time.
            Black swirls – a sudden
    Blanket of snow!
            And the blank
                At dawn, a maze
                Of silvery tell-tale trystings.

Ploughing Match
    If you come tonight
    Fisherman
    Take the track from the shore.
    The hill road
    Is reeling with malt-red ploughboys.

Clock
    We had the sun, stars, shadows.
    Today
    In Greta's house, a box
    Of numbers and wheels
    And cleek-cleek, click-clock, that insect
    Eating time at the wall.

Scarecrow
    A stick and tatter
    I lean into the sun's loom.

Envy
    I wish I was Andrew
    Standing
    With a bright shivering ring
    Beside that tall whiteness
    In the hushed barn
    Tonight
    When the minister urges the gold circlet from fingers to
                                  finger.

I would rather be Andrew
Than the laird
With a sideboard of silver plate
And silk hangings
And his seat in the parliament.

I would rather be
That ploughman
Than Lord Raglan on his stone snorting horse
Or Victoria stamped on a thousand coins.

Cat (to Dave Brock)
Swingler came in soft slippers.
My trout was needles
Before the knife could flash at the silver belly.

Swingler, pirate, with one patched eye
Unlocked
My golden cube of butter.

Swingler, exile, sits at my fire
All the six nights
The moon locks herself in her crystal cave.

My peats rage red on the winter stone.
Swingler sings.

The Laird's Garden

    Idle summer out (sang the bee)
    There are no jars
    In a cupboard of the House of Winter
    For drifters and dandlers and dreamers.

    Plunder the sun (mocked the butterfly)
    Smoulder. Save. Scheme.
    Mask-and-Glove take all, at last.

    See the gowned ladies and tulips going (said the bee)
    See, in the kirkyard
    The swirls of scented dust.

    The queen and her ingot-hoard (said the butterfly)
    Where are they
    When the Ice King
    Walks through the garden in his ancient armour?

Gravestone

    Suddenly a stone chirped
    Bella's goodness,
    Faithfulness,
    Fruitfulness,
    The numbers
    Of Bella's beginning and end.
    It sang like a harp, the stone!

    James-William of Ness
    Put a shilling
    In the dusty palm of the carver,
    Fifty years since.

Wind, snow, sun grainings.

The stone's a whisper now.
Soon
The stone will be silence.

Aurora
The Arctic girl is out tonight.
(Come to the doors.)
She dances
In a coat of yellow and green patches.
She bends
Over the gate of the stars.

What is she, a tinker lass?
Does she carry flashing cans
From the quarry fires?

I think
She's a princess in a silk gown
She holds (turning)
A bowl of green cut crystal.

Come to the doors!
She is walking about in the north, the winter witch.

Snow and Thaw
The first snowflake we called
'silver moth'.

We hailed the hill next morning –
Moby Dick!

Sun on sea,
blue silver blinding
mirrors.

The thaw, it was like an old filthy tramp
that had slept
in a ditch in downpours.

Mulled Ale
    The circus in Hamnavoe—
        Is that a fact,
            A man swallowing fire,
        A clown with patched cheeks?
            You should see my Jock
        After he's stuck the red-hot poker
    Five or six times in the ale pot.

Lessons
    Chants the young schoolmaster
        'First arithmetic. . .
        'Now spelling. . .
        'Now dates, kings and battles. . .'
    A butterfly loiters past the pane.
        Sam has a burning punished hand
    Because of a wind-flung flower and a cloud.

        'Now geography. . .'
    Book-bent heads. The first Arctic bird
    Crosses the window between ice and roses.

Wanderer
    I stood at ten doors in that island.

In the first door
I was shown the tooth of the dog.

In the second door
A stinking fish was put in my hand.

Senseless unprofitable babbling
In the third door.

A fiddle like a tortured cat
In the fourth door.

In the fifth door
A skull wrapped in a shawl, whisperings.

Sixth door, seventh door, eighth door
Barred.
I stood, a cancelled man, in the rain.

Twilight in the ninth door,
A star, a kiss.

When I come to the last door,
Take me, earth, soon
From their grain-gold sea-silvered hands.

Bird in the Lighted Hall

The old poet to his lute:
'Bright door, black door,
Beak-and-wing hurtling through,
This is life.
(Childhood lucent as dew,
The opening rose of love,
Labour at plough and oar,
The yellow leaf,
The last blank of snow.)
Hail and farewell. Too soon
The song is mute,
The spirit free and flown.
But you, ivory bird, cry on and on
To guest and ghost
From the first stone
To the sag and fall of the roof.'

Magi
(To Katia and Dominique)

JUNE 24: This day Karlson, Balth and I left the ship *Thor* secretly, and rowed in a small boat to one of a hundred islands. Sand burned, sun poured unbearable gold upon us.

JUNE 27: The map was plain in the mind of Balth. He drew it with his toe in the sand, and put an X where was the treasure. We have been to two islands. There is no word of the place.

JULY 1: Black and brown faces flee from our guns. But the forest is full of eyes. The water low in the skins. The night flies have bored me, arm and thigh.

AUGUST 18: How long we have lain in this village, in a hut, I do not know. The fever has branded us, all three. The ruined eyes of an old black man watched our shivering bones. Insects and honey he put in our mouths.

AUGUST 20: Karlson was first on his feet. He staggered like a drunk man. The old man laughed.

SEPTEMBER 29: Balth has left us, two days ago. Balth has taken the map that was in his mind. *They are a burden to me.* Did Balth say that? Yet he was a good companion. May he find the silver, may it sweeten his age. We are free and lost, Karlson and I.

OCTOBER 8: With Karlson and me, the only desire is to find a port with ships. Black hands point. *There, there the sails, beyond two rivers and a forest. . .*

NOVEMBER 21: One night lately was full of shapes of terror. Sleeping then, after sunset, I dreamed I was a child in Orkney, and I owned the whole world, corn and buttercup and rockpool, and the men and women and animals put looks of love on me and on each other.

Then to awake to the scarred face of Karlson, and mosquitoes, and smoke of a volcano, and a hidden mockery of parrots.

DECEMBER 1: The nights have been cold. Even the smaller peaks wear snow capes. In the port, one Spanish ship. A poster on the harbour-master's door: concerning absconded sailors, a reward, 3 familiar names. We drank the harbour-master's rum.

DECEMBER 8: We have nothing. We have no skill to catch wild creatures for the fire. The few rags on us are shameful compared to the comely nakedness of the savages. This is what the gold seekers have come to, penury and sickness.

DECEMBER 15: We saw Balth this day, talking with some brown men in a village. Their faces opened with white flashes. They chewed sticks. Balth gathered us into the company. *We are near the place*, he said. *The old map was useless. I have spoken with the Indians.* A black boy marked the dust with a star. Balth gave cuts of tobacco to the village men. *I knew we would come together here*, he said. *Perhaps tomorrow night, perhaps in nine nights or ten. It is worth the broken feet, a small betrayal.*

Sonnet: Hamnavoe Market

No school today! We drove in our gig to the town.
Grand-da bought us each a coloured balloon.
Mine was yellow, it hung high as the moon.
A cheapjack urged. Swingboats went up and down.

Coconuts, ice-cream, apples, ginger beer
Routed the five bright shillings in my pocket.
I won a bird-on-a-stick and a diamond locket.
The Blind Fiddler, the broken-nosed boxers were there.

The booths huddled like mushrooms along the pier.
I ogled a goldfish in its crystal cell.
Round every reeling corner came a drunk.

The sun whirled a golden hoof. It lingered. It fell
On a nest of flares. I yawned. Old Madge our mare
Homed through a night black as a bottle of ink.

Voyager
(To Dennis O'Driscoll)

On the third morning
We came to the whale acre.
No whales, the net
Surged with a galaxy of herring.
The raven, uncaged,
Fluttered over hidden islands.

On the eighth morning
A buttercup braid
Came down to meet us at a shore.
Her name was Gudrun.
A bluebell eye
Led us to hall and husband,
Harp, alehorn, fine flowers of flame.

No man, flame-fettered, finds fame
Or wrought gold.
On the twentieth morning
We dared the dark whirls,
Furious looms of sea.
There *Hawkwing* left us, whether
Broken in the salt shuttles
Or set on private pillage westward
We have not known.

We had small luck
With the holy crosses, the halls
Of Gaelic chiefs.
All were empty, all
Bore the famous brand marks.
Our fathers
Had been that way before.
Our fathers have left
Fine stories, burnt stones.
We sat hungry
Between a loch and a mountain
On the hundredth morning, under
The fourth moon.

Ragna, I write this
From an Irish village.
Are you still in the world,
I wonder
With your loom and quern and cheese-mould?
I am a gray humped man.
I had to learn new speech long ago.
I tend horses in a field.
After ten thousand mornings
Of rain, frost, larksong
How should I find a way back
To the waterfront of Trondheim?

Stars: A Christmas Patchwork

Innkeeper
I know you, Tomas the shepherd-boy.
A skin of wine, is it?
Tell them, no wine skins for hillmen. This ledger
Is crammed with their debts.
Take that cold face
Up among the cold stars.
Tell them, a new lamb
Might broach a barrel.
The rabble again –
Taxmen, yokels, tarts, soldiers.

Not another knock!

Census Official
Names and occupations in order.
    Isaac, tribe of David, fisherman
    Saul, tribe of David, goat-herd
    Joshua, tribe of David, baker
       (It's Caesar Augustus
       Wants your names, not me.
       Soon as I see
       The last of your mules and drums,
       It's the bright lights for me, pronto.
       Make your star on the parchment.)
    Jacob, lineage of David, brick-maker.

Soldier

No Miriam. I'm a soldier. It's midnight. The sentry
Locks the gate at midnight.
The colonel said,
Sharpen your swords, I want
Each eye cold as a star
Before the wakening of birds and children.

First King

Fix on one star, at last,
Any star
In the circling star blizzard.
That star will take you
Whithersoever,
Death and Birth and Love.

Herod

Tramps, dogs, children with palms, recognize Herod,
The skull with the sun-crown.
Kings would know a king, if the king
Wore a leper cloth.
I gaze, blind, through a golden mask.
Look for star-troubled strangers.
Under the merchant masks
They are kings and king-seekers.
Bring me word
Where the masquers unload their bales.

Bedtime Story, Bethlehem
> There was this old Chinaman
> (Once on a star time)
> A king yellow as a goldfish.
> He lived in a crystal palace.
> And one day came knocking on his door
> An Ebony king.
> And next noon came knocking
> An Ivory king.
> The three kings kissed. They crossed.
> They saddled mules. Their faces flushed with sunset.
> And then –
> *Wheest, the bairn's asleep.*

Second King
> A lantern at the gate, red as an apple.
> A village, clay houses.
> A lamp in every niche.
> We went on slowly, seeking
> The inn.
> (Sweet the wine bowl, bread, bason of water
> After such brandings of sun and sand.)
> At the inn
> One candleflame in a bottle, athwart
> A tumult of flushed mouths.
> In our chamber
> A star like a nail was the only light.

Priest

> Folded it is now, the dove,
> Furled, star-folded.
> Endless rain falls, the black floods are rising still.
> What hand
> Will take the branch from the dove's beak?

Third King

> We stand, three vagrants, at the last door.
> A black fist
> Lingers, a star, on withered wood.

Shepherd

> 'No wine.' He wouldn't part with a skin or a bottle.
> It was closing time.
> 'Come tomorrow,' the porter said.
> ('Bring a lamb,' said he.)
> 'The innkeeper's out of his wits
> With stars, soldiers, taxmen, foreigners, hill folk.'

126

Vinland

1
Wet shirt, breeches, kamiks
For a week
And a loud cough.
No blink of fire still
On the bleak
Unbroken circles of sea,
No singing throats
Between ship and shore.

2
The hungry raven
Astir in the basket. This
Is good, the bird
Eager
To be twelve masts up, turning!
That black hunger
Is smelling (we think)
Seeds and worms in the blank west.

3

Salt in the mouth,
The rage
Of north wind at morning,
Sodden crust,
Cold kissings of rain.
This unease
Is better than my Ragna at the hearth.

4

This heals heart,
On a blank stone westwards to cut
Such runes –
ICELANDERS
HUNTED THE GOLDEN WHALE
BEYOND HESPER

5

Too late for the rudder's turning
Back into history,
The old worn web,
King, lawman, merchant, serf.
The prow breaks thin ice
Into a new time.

6

He that can cup in the ear
Spidersong, dewfall
(Six weeks I hear only
Salt monotony)
Has heard, ahead,
Sea fingers fringing shore foam.

7

They will say next winter
At Greenland fires
'Leif Ericson went
The fool's voyage'.
A man will sing to a harp
'Heroes
Venture for more than bits of gold'.
An old woman will say
To girls at candle time
'It is that slut, the sea
Always
That has their hearts'.

Lighting Candles in Midwinter

Saint Lucy, see
Seven bright leaves in the winter tree

Seven diamonds shine
In the deepest darkest mine

Seven fish go, a glimmering shoal
Under the ice of the North Pole

Sweet St Lucy, be kind
To us poor and wintered and blind.

The Star to Every Wandering Barque
(for a 25th Wedding Anniversary)

Wave above wave – westward that night
The sea was a broken stair

In a house of menace, and never beacon or bell
To tell us where we were –

Near the great whirls, or close
To crag or reef or shallow (God knows where).

Above, thick-woven cloud. Beneath
The skull-strewn dragon lair.

How long, how late, since the ship
Had cleared the harbour bar

We made no reckoning soon. Our skipper plied
Ship-wit, sea-care.

(Will the heart keep tryst?
Does the dove, branch-burdened, quest through the
                                   perilous air?)

Precious the cargo,
Urgent the hunger that drew it from shore to shore.

Deep in the hold
The jars of love we bore.

All who trade in that freightage
Dread the devourings of time, and salt, and tare.

How could we have doubted?
Like a lantern in a barn door,

Like the roof-furled familiar dove,
Upon our voyage hung the homing star.

Orkneymen at Clontarf, AD 1014

What are you doing here, Finn?
(I ask myself that.)
Today, Good Friday, the ox in Stronsay
Tears sweet grass
Beside an idle plough, the women
Go between kirk and bread-board.
Panis angelicus sing
The priest and the boys.

Sigurd is the name of our earl.
His mother the witch
Wove our black banner.
That raven croaks above the host.
Whoever bears the bird of victory
Drinks tonight in dark halls.
Now Sigurd alone
Offers the raven to a sackcloth sun.

'If you go to Ireland,' she said
'Speak to the holy men
With their prayers and candles,
Not to the little kings
Offering bits of battle silver.'
That's what my mother said, in Westray.
I'm young. What do I want with a psalter?
The silver pieces
Will buy an ox for next ploughtime.

I forget the name of the saint
That saved my grandfather
Under a burning wall of Paris one summer.
Whatever your name, white one
I am grandson
To old Olaf, that you kept from torrents of lead and tar
One day in the Seine.
I intend to light a candle to you.

I bought the horse in Dublin.
Seven times
It reared against horn and shield-wall.
Now that it's hide and bone, that nag,
And tatters of blood
I am walking back to the town.
At the river mouth
The proud Minch-trampler is moored.

Coming to Ireland
We stopped first at Barra.
A cold week, snow in the ale.
Coming to Ireland
About some royal mix-up or other
We stopped at Man.
I devoted an April day to bright edges.
Coming to Ireland
We have stopped at a noisy fairground, Clontarf.
The revellers
Go and come in red masks and patches.

When they said, *Rolf is dead*
Under a hoof
I said, 'Fare on, Rolf.
It goes well with you, friend.
Flesh-unfastened,
A swift swallowflight soon
To the Hall of Heroes.'
Then I turned and gave release
To three Irish axemen.

We drank thick ale in Galloway.
Brave boasting there –
Battles, blood, wall-breaching, booty.
Now the glory is come
There is no ditch anywhere
I would not creep into,
Sharing a mushroom with tramp and slut.

Sven swore, in Hoy, he would never
Come into Ireland.
'A place of enchantment, Ireland.'
Yet he sang with us at the rowing-bench
Down the broken coastline of Scotland.
Here
A white star has broken on Sven's brow.

In Rousay this sunset
Under Scabra
Men will be lifting lobsters.
A girl at a rockpool
Is shaking out yellow hair.
If I do not get back from this battle
Tell the brewer at Kierfea
We have found a quieter alehouse,
Free drink, no hangovers.

William and Mareon Clark:
First Innkeepers in Hamnavoe

1   THE OPENING OF THE TAVERN, 1596

Johnsmas. The noon light clear and hard,
　　He bade Mareon, his ship-shape wife
　　　Unlatch the new oak door.
No lingering man or beast in the yard.
　　　Not a foot crossed the sanded floor
　　To chair and flagon, platter and knife.
　　　　A barrel seethed in one corner, the best March ale.
　　　　　Five hams on the hook, well cured in winter
　　　　　　　　　　　　　　smoke.
From the kitchen, a fragrance and crispness of bread.
Beyond, clean bolsters and blankets spread.
　　　　A house of keeping it was for far-come folk,
　　With turf and driftwood to feed the welcoming flame.
Four days of silence. Nobody came.
　　　Then William said, 'Goodwife, I see
　　　　Bad counsel I had from lawyer and shipman and
　　　　　　　　　　　　　　earl
　　　　Anent the lease of this inn
Here on a barren spit of shore.
　　　We will flourish here like the winter whin.
It's road and tinker rags for you and me'. . .
The next day (sea lash, gull whirl, gale)
　　　They saw a Frenchman anchor and furl
　　From the outer Atlantic roar.

William and Mareon kept an anxious silence.
  Knockings and strange shouts soon at the gale-
                             shook door.
    A brig blunders bayward, anchors, and furls
    Behind the two sheep islands.
Mareon's board brims over with bread and ale,
    With gold of honey-jar, pinkness of hams.
        What sea-gray faces now – Balticmen? Danes?
        The counter rang with strange-carved coins.
    Then the sun drew qualms
    Of dancing light from ear-rings, silver buttons, flagon-
                             whorls.

2 *SICKNESS*

William, the skull
No mistake. I counted thrice. The brewster in
    Stenness delivered *six*, not seven barrels ale.

William, the worm and the skull
Provided for. First winter here I sent for the
    lawyer. 'You won't starve, Mareon.' Quill
    and parchment and wax. The will.

William, the shroud, the worm and the skull
The sun. Ugh, your cobwebs and crushed spider!
    Breckness wind in the face. That restores me.
    Flood in the Sound – curve and brake and splash of a
                             gull.

William, hands crossed, the shroud, the worm and the skull
Has she blown out the lamp? set traps? locked door
                             and till?

William, the dark one, hands crossed, the shroud, the worm
and the skull
We all go under the hill.

William, the weeping, the dark one, hands crossed, the shroud,
the worm and the skull
I repent me of (heartily) world-wickedness, my
   part in such, all things done ill.

William, last candle, the weeping, the dark one, hands crossed,
the shroud, the worm and the skull
It does well.

3   IN MEMORIAM

Four hundred years since you both
. Went, sundered, into the dark,
Hearts and hearthstone cold,
   William and Mareon Clark.

Search for a stone in the kirkyard –
Nothing. Never a mark.
No one knows where your bones lie,
   William and Mareon Clark.

Even the inn you built
To hustle about the work
Of welcome and keeping, is vanished,
   William and Mareon Clark.

Your door stood open wide
From the rising of the lark
To the pole of night, to all men,
   William and Mareon Clark.

You gathered about your fires
The crew of the wintered barque
From Bergen, or Brest, or Lubeck,
 William and Mareon Clark.

Did Rome and Geneva strive
For the helm of the storm-tossed kirk
Even in this quiet haven,
 William and Mareon Clark?

Tired, you'd put out the lamp,
Cover the fire, and hark!
A scatter of hooves on the cobbles,
 William and Mareon Clark.

You did not live to see
On the steep dyked westward park
The merchants' houses rising,
 William and Mareon Clark;

Tall houses hewn from granite,
Piers on the tidal mark,
Yawl and cobble noust-gathered,
 William and Mareon Clark.

Your first eyes never saw
Boys from the crofts embark
For the Davis Straits and the whale-fling,
 William and Mareon Clark

Nor saw them come back in August,
Sovereigns sewn in each sark,
Salt men urgent for barley,
  William and Mareon Clark.

Eighteenth-century wars,
The herring shoal and the shark
Dowered that shore with silver,
  William and Mareon Clark.

Eighteenth-century wars,
Doubloon and kroner and mark
Made later taverners rich,
  William and Mareon Clark.

Graham and Gow and Millie –
You never drew the cork
For hero, pirate, spaewife,
  William and Mareon Clark.

Nothing. You cannot hear us.
Two names, quilled and stark
On a lawyer's parchment, ghostings –
  William and Mareon Clark.

Forgive this deluge of words,
First townsfolk, wherever you ark.
I have cut you dove-marks on stone –
  WILLIAM and MAREON CLARK.

Countryman

Come soon. Break from the pure ring of silence,
A swaddled wail

You venture
With jotter and book and pencil to school

An ox man, you turn
Black pages on the hill

Make your vow
To the long white sweetness under blessing and bell

A full harvest,
Utterings of gold at the mill

Old yarns, old malt, near the hearthstone,
A breaking of ice at the well

Be silent, story, soon.
You did not take long to tell

TRYST IN EGILSAY

The great drama at the heart of the Orkney story is the meeting on Easter Monday 1117 of the two earls of Orkney – cousins – Magnus Erlendson and Hakon Paulson. What had been planned as a peace-meeting ended in the execution of Earl Magnus; the events that led up to it have the power and inevitability of Greek tragedy. The murdered earl soon became St Magnus the Martyr; the murderer became one of the greatest and justest of the Orkney earls. 'So shines a good deed in a naughty world'.

The story of Magnus and Hakon is magnificently told in *The Orkneyinga Saga*, written down in Iceland about AD 1300.

This seven-fold poem celebrates the events of that April day as seen by some of the people on the island.

EARL HAKON

I reason with Norway, 'Here are the two earls
In the great hall of Orkney.
The stone hawk over the door is withered.
I pass from room to disordered room.
I wait for a dove-sign from the lord Magnus.'

I walked on the hill of the farmers.
Ploughs broken, sickles rust-eaten,
Rats at the seed sack in the barn.

I came to the yard of the shipwrights.
The peaceful strakes for fishing-boats
Are gone to the swelling hull of a longship.
One shipwright spoke with masons and a priest.

143

I came to the chamber of the women.
The daughters of music had twisted mouths.
Some sewed an altar cloth.
One woman stood apart, and wept.
In the chamber of the skippers
They traced viking routes on a chart.
A few discussed, in secret, a *stone ship*.

Then, in the chapel, this cry
That they may take the wings of the morning . . .

Magnus housed long, in a seagirt cell, westwards.

This can never be good, a cloven earldom,
Bad governance, the folk
fallen into faction, insolence, orisons.
I too would have a sheaf carved on the lintel.
Therefore to Egilsay we have sailed,
The prows of my eight ships beaked like falcons.

HELMSMAN

Off Scilly I first swung an oar
Going then to Africa for gold, a boy.

I am not that old now
But I've been as far as Greenland.
Ice gnawed at the hull with green teeth.

I think there may be land further west.
Only the eye of the sun sees it.
An Icelander, Leif
Plucked grapes on that shore.
The old sailors in Shetland say
Leif had too much of his own treading
The day he stained his mouth with Vinland juice.

I went with Swedes down a river in Russia.
The domes of Byzantium! My eyes dazzled.
There were too many Norskies in that town.
Their axes a hedge about the Emperor.

What am I doing, rowing gentry
Through a sea of glass *ad insulam ecclesiae*?
Yes, I have smatterings of Latin
As well as French, Scots, Spanish.
I like best the Greek words for *sea*.

Phew! that wave made a tangled web of the oars.

I didn't know Finn and Hold, those lairds,
Cared all that much about kirks.
What, there? Sea bell on a hidden rock?
Swing the prow of *Dove* a point to west.
It's the bell of the little kirk,
A slow small joy over the black and gray furrows.

THE KILLERS

Now they go down, laughing, to the shore.
Now they shout for food, for ale clamour.
But truly this face and that, gray-masked.

Yea, and the fire gray embers, the pots
With raw meat on the bone and cold dregs.

Lifolf would not cook that day, Lifolf
Walked under the crag with red hands
And never cook wore such a coat,
Sewn gold and scarlet from throat to hem
And seven buttons of carved ivory.

Then Sigurd blew strong breath on the embers
But the fire died on the stones.
Would they break down a door for kindling?
The sport and the laughter
Were dead in them suddenly like the fire.
And one said, 'The peasant will need his door in winter.'

One said, 'Every man drinks his own cup of death.
Whatever road he takes, forest or firth
Or mountain path or moor scratchy with whins,
At the end of the road is the cup brimming with shadows.
He must hold over his gray mouth
The inverted cup to the uttermost black drop.'
In the church the Mass of the dead is sung.

The earl said, 'Go now in order into the ship.'

146

The earl that had drunk the cup said nothing.
A day and a night, nothing.
Nor priest nor peasants came about that silence.
With the evening star, the soul began its singing.

THE DEATH OF MAGNUS

What's this? I'm bidden to a great feast?
But here I stand, lost
On a dark moor, and I can hardly move
For the heavy coat-of-state on my shoulders.

Men pass me on the moor. They wear masks
Of wolf and of raven.
They *seem* to pass me, then come about,
They stand in a yelping circle.
They are the ones appointed, I think,
To bring the earl to the feast.

How have I, of all men, deserved a feast?
The islands are in trouble.
Fire in the thatch, blood on the shore,
Their tables and cupboards empty,
Weeping at every doorstep .
And I who am set over this people
Bidden to bring them with me to the banquet.

The women go by with clay pots to the spring.
Where is the golden bowl?

A man stands before you, Magnus.
He is poor. He's in tears.
The axe shakes in his hands.
The spring morning is very cold.
Put your coat-of-state about him, Magnus.

Quick – let the silver cord be loosed.

The dark waters rise up into my soul.
Here's your ship of death, Magnus.
Those bright ones? They ferry you over to the Feast.

THE EGILSAY PRIEST

Sun wakes me. I go into the cold kirk.
I light candles, set out wine and bread.
A boy might come, sticky-eyed.
Now I am another, vested, with clean hands.

Otherwise, Petrus, this is a poor place.
One might come, grumbling – some old man
Had the last hunger on him.
One might come – 'Thord, ploughman,
And Gerd my lass are bespoke.
And the dowry, one ox.'
I must set seal, unbreakable, to that pledge.

One might come. In April Erling
Hammered a new cradle.
Now the bairn's on board. Let three water drops
Signify the great deluge
That bore, brimming, the ark and all creation.

But that the seven gifts in my keeping
Put the beauty of heaven on this people,
I'd be better dusting parchments in Trondheim.

One came, at sunset. 'Sir, two fine ships
Are anchored off the ness.'

Another, 'A lord, cold, is knelt in the kirk.'

Let the bishop see to the lords of Orkney.
That one golden bird
Should brush this poor island and drop
A splendid plume, is a throw of chance.
If the man is there when I light the Mass candles
He'll have greeting like any cleaver of the clay.

THE MEN OF EGILSAY

All morning on the sea, cold, with creels.
And not one lobster.
Home now, and the fire out, and not a hunk of bread
On table, or cupboard, or griddle.
I'll knock that Sigrid black and blue. I will.

The plough stottering after the ox since dawn,
I stottering after the plough.
The house empty and cold as a cave.
Not one baked sillock* to eat. Oh, my good Ragna!

* *sillock – young coalfish*

I'll tell you where they are, the women.
They're all in the kirk, kneeling.
Don't bide indoors. The lords of Orkney are here.
They're throwing silver about them like rain.
Forget the fish and the bannocks.
Enough shillings to drink the ale house dry.

The lords walk in order to the moor.
Their speech is like old carved stones.

One of the lords sat in the kirk all night . . .

Why should the lords choose Egilsay
For their corn dance? Why not?
We have just ploughed and seeded the furrows.
A third of our barley is for their longships,
A third for Bergen, the king's granary there.
In a masque there's always a death,
Always a hero, always a clown, and women keening.

Look – the shape of Ingi against the sunset!
And Thora, Sigrid, Ragna, Sunniva, Maurya.
Return to us, Magnus, laden with cornstalks.

THE TWO TINKERS

'If I had their seven silver cups
I'd be richer than the king in Bergen.'
– A drag and a clang like chains on you always.

'But if I had two silver cups
We wouldn't be poor all winter.'
– No sleep for you under the stars
For fear Slok the thief
Might have the cups from under your skull.

'The priest is lifting – look – the silver cup.'

– All the world can drink from that cup,
The two tinkers that we are,
And the lord Magnus with the heavy folds about him
And Aud the skipper
And the fisherman with a bunch of herring
And the wife with a loaf from the fire.
The priest drinks for all, high and low.

'If I had four silver cups, or five, or six,
It would mean this:
A great hall and a fire in every room,
And a garden with an oak and a falcon,
And a ship in the west,
All the people kissing the dust as we ride past.'

– What are a thousand silver cups
And you a dead man
And no thirst or quenching in you at all –
A clay pitcher fallen on a stone?

On they went, one April day, through an island.
Mugs – best tin – three for a penny.

FORESTERHILL

In the spring and early summer of 1990 I was a patient at Foresterhill, the Aberdeen Royal Infirmary. To pass the time, I worked on a sequence of poems, imagining a medieval monastic beginning for Foresterhill.

I was trying to express some gratitude, too, to the surgeons, doctors, and nursing staff.

I finished the draft of the sequence at Balfour Hospital in Orkney, before coming home.

Cutting Down Trees
    In a clearing of trees
        (Cut down twenty trees)
    Here let it be built, the hut
            Near a well, with a hearthstone.
    We can spare two brothers
    One with healing in his hands
    One with a psalter interleaved with herbs.
    It may be, the sick man
    That fled from stones into the heart of the forest
        Will seek the fire
    And will be there still when morning sifts through the
                                                    branches.

Pirates
The pirates drifted between Benahie and the woods,
The sea bandits
That put knives in this net and that
And prowled under the castle roots,
Lewis-men or Danes.
Farmers drove cattle into byres,
Set a night watch on a fold here and there,
The provost had a drum sounded at the Don-mouth.

The wolf-man, trapper
Saw their prints
And fire marks in twenty places in the forest
And a trail of blood.

'Yes,' said the brother in the hospice door
'A foreigner with a sea wound on him,
And we put oil and leáves on his thigh.'

Architect
Macher, architect, built merchants' houses.
Last month, a villa at Dee-mouth for a skipper's widow,
Five crowns in purse for that work.
Soon, in farms, the fever-fire.
This mason, master of the granite hewing, squaring, last
                              pure chiselling, cold star glitters,
'There must be a cool place, infirmaria,
Pines that have lately known snow
Where they bide till the roses of sickness wither.'
See, this drawing on a hide: *Macher made this* inscribed.

Wreck

A stack near Colliston of the yawls.
The *Schwartz*, Lübeck, wrecked there,
Cargo, Rhenish, heavy wax at the bungs,
       for chamberlains at Holy Rood, twenty-one casks.

One sailor in the hospice, salt-scarred.
With leaves, distillations of herbs restored
He might yet stretch a sail beyond Kiel.

Lowlanders

This one broke an ankle in a furrow.
This one lost teeth fighting.
A rash huntsman,
This one took the boar's fang, at Insch.
Another hand poisoned with salmon hooks.

Knife, lint, essences from phial and phial.
We give them back to wind and sun.

Is there war in the mountains westward?
We heard of Saxon horsemen
At Tummel, the heads turned north.
We have seen ploughboys
At barn-gables, singing war songs,
Women urging, women
Dragging the fools back by their coat-tails.

The stockmen drive herds west and north.

At Foresters' Hill is no provision
For a festival of wounds.

Healer

Gift of wholeness, blossoming, the dance
Of air, stone, rain.

I think of Eck, his blundering
With pen and scroll – such blots – in the library.
No, he could not wash a floor
But the bucket was upset.
The voice of Eck a crow at Matins and Vespers.
Weed the herb garden, Eck. Weeds only
Infested the plot.
We must send Eck back soon
To his father and the fishing boat at Catterline.

In the diversity of gifts, for Eck
Nothing, a stone on his palm.

At Foresters' Hill, our infirmary there
Eck found rare roots in the burn
We hadn't known before.
Virtue flowed from Eck's fingers
Into abcess and lesion.
The lepers cry, 'We'll have Eck for bandaging, brothers.'

So we may see, dear people
Blessings may break from stone, who knows how.

Fee

A horseman going in and out of the trees,
He ties bridle to branch.

A purse from the tapestry coat,
Spanish leather.
A gold coin, drop of sunsweat
Offered to the doorkeeper.
For healing of my father, last harvest
Who died however in the first snow.

How should Eck know
The fee from a hard round of butter, a frozen honey-
                                                        splash?

The infirmarian:
Your honour, that treasure may not rot the fabric of our house
– And may your sire
Have inherited riches beyond price – grant us at Foresterhill
                                                        rather
The rock with watersprings under it,
A field where Mags and Moondrift our cows
May yield us gold of butter and mead
For restoration of sick guests.

Pilgrim
    'Who went quickly among the trees
    Disturbing that blackbird?'

    Finnbar stopped here at sunset
    Finnbar from Pluscarden
    Going on to Walsingham, Compostella.
    We put bandages on his feet,
    A crust in his bowl.

    Finnbar has sat so long
    In the scriptorium
    How will his white feet endure
    The Pyrenees and the Alps?

Castellan
    A man from Dunnotar stopped at our gate
    Going from salmon runs in the Spey,
    Drops from his net and hooks, like gray blood.

    'Cough, ague, bone-break, fever –
    Why do you waste your days
    On death-farers?
    Let them take their bruisings
    To the swart door of the skull.
    Your mercies
    Deny a clean surge, the dance in the teeming estuaries.'

    The castellan, laughing
    Put five fish on the doorkeeper's plate.

157

Lux Perpetua
Three axemen from the woodyard. They mark
A tree here and there. Snow
Comes shivering from black branches.
A drawing on a scroll.

A face beside a dead candle, cold.
It is not good
To hurry him in at the earth door.
Let him lie three nights
In this stark cell
Glister of oil on eyes and mouth
The hands folded
New candles lighting head and feet
And the chanting *Lux perpetua*

The builders will build in this clearing
A waiting room for the poor soul
Before it whispers for entrance at the door of purification.

Beeman
We have Alisdore with us, master of the bees.

Alisdore from Echt tired of a wife
Trading his golden combs
At the haberdasher's for ribbons,
Saying to a cadger
'A sun-oozing box for seven salt herring.'
She might feed the pig honey, that woman.
There's a stickiness
In the cups, on chair and on blanket.
One old May
She had a sweetness, that lass, no hive could match.

Alisdore brought a swarm from Echt
And built hives in a clearing
Thick heather blossom on three sides.

Village folk hoarse in the throat
Tilt faces to a gold-dripping spoon.

A Scroll
Sun faileth not
    Pouring our cornstalks and honey
       From the golden jar.

Moon never fails, the shifting silver of the plate
    A-jostle with fish.

Stars not fail, that fleece and cargoes
    Be ushered home under Hesper.

*

The lantern at our gatepost will soon be out.
The candles over our beds of suffering, they will be cold
                             wax in time.
The refectory fire a smoke-blackened stone.

*

A holy man had written:
Prayers, charities, alms, blessings
These be the little flames
Outlasting diamond and emerald and the star-in-the-
                                   granite.

Homily

We go into distances, near or far, each man to his own
                                                    bourne.

In childhood, all is green and good,
Trees, horses, stones, stars, flowers.
                        (There is only the garden,
                            never gate or a road
                            beyond the garden.)

There comes a call in the night, in youth, a summons
                            purer than music,
                        deeper than truth itself.
We go out into wind and a few stars.

In the morning we are on a desolate road
(Where is the woman, keeper of fire, the children,
The house on its firm rock, the flock on the hill?
There and not there: shadows.)

The voice is all delight to us still
In the first lingering flakes of age.

The sun sets on our labouring urgency.
We hurry to find an inn
With fire and bottle, fish and bread.
It thickens to black snow.
Breath, heart are snagged with nets of blizzard.
But there is no lamp of welcome at midnight.

Cry of a torrent under a broken bridge, far on.

160

What will the dayspring show?

Look for no company of goodly folk
No fellow pilgrims on that road.
Loneliness is all
And the bitter fruit of the selfhood of each man –
Shame, regret, fear, sorrow, rage.

We are beyond the last scars of snow
And there the fires begin.

                           *

　We brothers put ourselves here, at the door
　And in the choir, with music
　And at the board with a few loaves
　And at the beds with candles
　And one on the road outside, at midnight, with a
                                                   lantern

　Should a soul go past bereft and weeping.

Water Casks
　　Rain after drought – it gargled
　　All a night in pipe and water barrels.

　　　What did the downpours sing?

　　'A barrel for the kirn and the still . . .
　　One for washing wounds . . .
　　One for the herb-yard when a wind blows the dust . . .
　　One for the horse, he curls black lips at the end of the
　　　　　twelfth furrow, he slurps on the brigstone, he strikes
　　　　　　　out galaxies with the hoof, the eye rolls like a
　　　　　　　　　　thunderball . . .
　　One for Fergus, may he make the flagstones to shine in
　　　　　　　　　　　the chapel . . .
　　One to mirror in a meniscus the young ice of the moon,
　　　　the star wheel, rose of dawn, before we come and make
　　　　　　　a disturbance with bucket and bowl . . .
　　One for small jars to mingle with the altar wine . . .'

A New Ward
　　'Another clearing, higher up?
　　Cut down fifty trees!'

　　The forester at his door, red in the face.
　　Downturned faces of three brothers.

　　'Would you drive the deer from the forest?
　　What will they say, the burghers?
　　What will Dunnotar say
　　If the stag climbs into Lochnagar?

162

Would you have no chanting in the dells next spring,
Blackbird and linnet?
Have the little black pigs of the forest done you harm?
Must the charcoal men starve?'

The woodman shuts his door against them.

The woodman went up with a honed axe in winter.
Snow fell shattering from boughs in fifty sudden
                                        dazzlements.

Cattle Thieves
    Rievers were out before sundown. Rievers
    Were out. Rievers from Mearns or westward
    Astride shaggy colts
    Poured down the hill, wild shadows
    And turned and were off
    Driving cattle from Kirkton and Tarty
    And the night full of rage, laughter, urging.
    What will we do with one thief
    Thrown from horseback, his leg askew?

    The bailiff twisted straw, looked for a tree.

    We sent Nechtan with a lantern.
    He carried the lad, a sack of pain, into dawnlight.

    Seven weeks on, we think
    The boy will go gravewards rolling like a tipsy sailor
                                through streets in Arbroath,
    A stranger always to horses and horned cattle.

Comings and Goings

Where do you go from here, traveller?
    Ruddy in the cheek again, I go seeking a harvest fee
                                        in Echt.

Do you go on far, traveller?
    To Catterline, with a cart to buy fish, now the fever
                                       has left me.

You will leave us so soon, traveller?
    Yes, I can hammer nails again in the boatyard in
                    Torry, bright and true and ringing.

A bleak day to cross the hill, traveller.
    A shepherd with an eye-patch sees but half the ewe-
                                graving snow.

We are not innkeepers, traveller, and charge board.
    Take this silver, Charon will have his due soon.

You must bide with us longer, seaman.
    Cargo me with oil and bread, father, against the
                    troubling of the bar at sunset.

What do you seek at this door, traveller?
    The word is, you have good leaves for toothache.

Returns

There is no compulsion, those
Who've been made whole
Can chop logs beyond the burn.

Our garden has plenty of roots and stones
For hands renewed
If hands and hearts are willing, only.

An old patient can call in cow to byre.

If a man has ten gold pieces
He might leave one (scripturally)
That would build a new chamber of wholeness among
                                         the trees
If the forester is agreeable.

It is sufficient
To say *Ave* and *Gloria* in the hospice chapel.

BRODGAR POEMS

The poem sees the work on this Neolithic stone circle as lasting two or three generations at least. 'She who threw marigolds over you . . . is a crone now with cindery breath . . .'
It may have been a meeting-place, a temple, a hymn to the sun and the stars.
Even as a civilisation is being established, its history is beginning to crumble. Strange boats from time to time sailed along the horizon, going north and west, threatening the precarious settlements.
But a circle has no beginning or end. The symbol holds. People in AD 2000 are essentially the same as the stone-breakers and horizon-breakers of 3000 BC.

The Third Stone
   The third pit is dug. Stone
   Sips the brim of darkness.
   The stone tree
   Will have tonight its star-leaves.

The Fifth Stone
   Hunter, don't give all your strength to the wild boar.
   A stone waits in Vestrafiold.

The Eighth Stone
   Disturb the roots, let the worm
   Seek a new stair.
   I hear shouting between the hills.

166

The Ninth Stone
    After this snow, the ninth stone.

The Eleventh Stone
    They say, never such loveliness between the lochs
    As that girl.
    In the pause between two stones
    She became a swan.
    She flew from us into sunset and stars.

The Thirteenth Stone
    We have heard, men
    Who have no knowledge of stones
    Are in ships.
    Save us, stone, from the harps in the west.

The Fourteenth Stone
    We said to the children,
    'At last the stones
    Will be like the first little rose, that opens beside the
                                                    burn.'
    'It will be like a spider's web
    With the dew on it.'
    Those children
    Were at the dragging of the fourteenth stone.

The Seventeenth Stone
   They go, the old crones
   Plucking heather
   To thatch the huts before winter.
   'Swan', they called one.
   'Daffodil', one, once.
   (The old men laugh)
   'Dew of morning.'
   'Butterfly.'
   A new stone watches them.
   They stoop, here and there, snatching.

The Nineteenth Stone
   The girls hold buttercups under their chins.
   'You will make the best cheeses.'
   A cow cries to be milked.
   The girls turn,
   They shower the newest stone with buttercups.

The Twentieth Stone
   Today, the young men, a score
   Levered from Vestrafiold
   The tallest stone, a star-raker.
   Ale-skins were dry
   Before the arrival of the stone-dresser.

The Twenty-third Stone
   Those ships on the horizon
   Are made of trees.
   The bog has eaten our forest.
   What are our curraghs but thin water flies?
   Stones, one more than last winter,
   Guard us from the foreign ships.

168

The Twenty-fourth Stone: Thunder
  Hammer on the hills,
  Black stammer!
  The cloud, a fistful of flashes,
  Cut a stone forehead.
  The stones, against the purple sky,
  Danced.
  After the thunder, sun.
  One stone has a red wound.

The Twenty-sixth Stone
  The man from the shipwreck said
  'We have seen stone clusters
  Far south, in Lewis, Wessex, Brittany.'
  That seaman
  Withered soon in the circle of the hills.

The Twenty-seventh Stone
  Sunset, midsummer. Who
  Reads the riddle,
  The dance, the torches of celebration?
  None.
  Corn whispers, wonders, urges. *Ah, gold kiss.*

The Twenty-eighth Stone
  Curlew-cry
  Across a clean stone face.
  The old stones have lichen beards.

The Thirtieth Stone
  Hill in the west, Mother
  Vestrafiold,
  We thank you for one more child, this strong guardian.

The Thirty-first Stone
   Fish-net, fleece wheel, quern, milk-kirn,
   Hollow of wet clay
   Standing all night in a nest of flame,
   Be this new stone a friend to all.

The Thirty-second Stone
   She who threw marigolds over you, stone,
   A child,
   She is a crone now with cindery breath.
   You, stone,
   Two younger stones curve beyond you.

The Thirty-third Stone
   Lift from us the curse of time,
   Birth, blossoming, cinder breath.
   A beautiful stone
   Is walking today across the hill
   Under a splurge of larks.

The Thirty-fourth Stone: The Pipes
   This new stone is acquainted with pipe music
   Grave and pure –
   Not shrieks from a split grassblade.

The Thirty-seventh Stone
   It may be, the stones are attentive
   To first cry and last cry,
   The thunder
   In the heart of a young man in April.
   Release us, stone,
   From the three anguishes.

170

The Fortieth Stone
  This stone walked through the hills
  Between cornstalk and fish.
  What, the men groaned and bled
  Clearing a way for the stone?
  One skull, in truth,
  Has been laid bare by the eagles.
  I tell you, the men danced.
  They stretched their mouths with praise, laughter.

The Forty-first Stone
  That yellow row of skulls on the shelf
  Saw one ship only.
  The shrunken mouths at the aleskin,
  They counted seven.
  Men from the sea
  Took a hundred fleeces
  At Skaill, the year of the fortieth stone.

The Forty-second Stone
  Thunder among the hills.
    'The wild Kierfiold horses?'
    'Waves against Yesnaby?'
  Twenty men left at sunrise
  With rollers, oxen, ropes, a jar of ale.

The Forty-third Stone
  'The new stone, broken and dressed
  It could be a house
  For falconer and first child.'
  The chatterer beside the small sun on the hearth,
  That ignorance,
  We drove out into the stars and snow.

The Forty-fifth Stone
What broke from the cloud? Rain, sun, the hawk.
A stone walks under a cloud slowly.

The Fiftieth Stone: Plague and Pillage
And if the pustules, the fevers
Fired
This people again, like dry heather
Or if a foreign sailor
Stood in every door, some dawn
And the circle not closed . . .
Fowlers, fishers, farmers
Have not been quarrymen
Now, seven years.
In Vestrafiold a stone waits, half-hewn.

The Fifty-second Stone
Look, a small boy with hook and limpet shell
Lying in the reeds.
The swan does not care.
The tall stone, if it cares, has care
Beyond the span of our caring.
Take seaweed from the boy's mouth.

Index of first lines